OUR
Ebenezer

— A JOURNEY OF FAITH, FAMILY, AND FARMING —

PAM AND JOHN DYSINGER

TEACH Services, Inc.
PUBLISHING
www.TEACHServices.com • (800) 367-1844

Copyright © 2016 Pam Dysinger

Copyright © 2016 TEACH Services, Inc.

ISBN-13: 978-1-4796-0635-1 (Paperback)

ISBN-13: 978-1-4796-0636-8 (ePub)

ISBN-13: 978-1-4796-0637-5 (Mobi)

Library of Congress Control Number: 2016916707

Unless otherwise indicated, all Scripture quotations are from the King James Version (KJV).

Published by

TEACH Services, Inc.
P U B L I S H I N G
www.TEACHServices.com • (800) 367-1844

Special Thanks

There have been many people who have "lifted up our hands" along this faith journey, but we want to give special thanks to our *parents!*

We know it wasn't easy for you to watch us struggle, and we know there were times when you probably thought we had lost our minds, but we are very appreciative that you gave us the space and freedom to pursue God with all our hearts. The ways you supported and encouraged us were many, and we are eternally grateful!

We are afraid to start mentioning the names of the many others who have been a great help to us, for fear of leaving people out, so we just say, "Praise God" and "Thank you" to all our friends and family who have inspired and strengthened us along the way.

Contents

A Note from Pam

"No," I said. "I am not a writer." And that was the truth. But the Lord was not willing to take "no" for an answer. The book you hold in your hands is the result of God's persistent calling to my heart. He also used others who told us that we really should share what the Lord has done for our family.

Bountiful Blessings Farm is the result of God's never-failing guidance and patient teaching through the many different circumstances He has placed in our pathway. He has sustained us through extremely difficult times, and carried us when we were unable to navigate on our own. Ultimately, He gave us the faith to press forward, and then He rewarded us for choosing to trust His faithfulness through it all.

John is the writer in our family, but he has been far too busy to write. So, of course, I decided that there would be no book. Sometimes, though, I asked myself, "What title would I choose for a book if I ever did write one?"

The very day after I emphatically affirmed to a long-distance friend that I could never write any kind of a book, we had a guest speaker at church. He chose 1 Samuel 7:12 as his Scripture. The context explains the impossible odds against the Israelites in their desperate war with the Philistines. The victory God gave them was beyond anything they could have imagined. After the battle Samuel set up a stone "and called the name of it Ebenezer, saying, Hitherto hath the Lord helped us."

On that Sabbath day I knew that the book I was never going to write would be titled *"Our Ebenezer."*

Over the years many different people encouraged us to write down all that God has done for us in our faith journey towards country living. Time was the problem. We just didn't have time. The burden to write rested more heavily on my heart than on my husband's. The words "Go . . . tell them what great things the Lord has done for you and how He has had compassion on you" (Mark 5:19) often came to mind, and with increasing urgency. At last I laid aside my flimsy excuses and began. I trusted that if this task was assigned by my Heavenly Father, He would give time and ability to complete it.

When you sit down to begin writing about an important part of your life, it makes you re-evaluate all of the lessons and blessings the Lord has put in your path. The greatest blessing of my life is being the wife of John Dysinger. For twenty-nine years we have faced life's challenges together. The Lord has taught us lessons, stretched our faith, and helped us to trust Him more and more fully. John's willingness to follow God's leading, no matter what the cost, opens the way for heaven's plans to succeed. In a "take charge" world, John is learning the art of waiting on God and following His directions.

My life's highest calling began with the birth of Kirsten after four years of marriage. She was followed by her four brothers: Jonathan, Joshua, Zack, and Caleb. Each of our precious children taught me many lessons about myself and about our loving Father in Heaven. Each child adds much to our shared journey of "experimental religion."

As our children shared in the "blood, sweat and tears" that laid the foundation of our farm, I often struggled with the fear that I was failing them by spending so little time with the school books. If the strawberries needed picking, that was school! If there was a problem to solve, then solving that problem was school too! It was a little like the "olden days." My children learned to work—to work hard—and to pray for wisdom while they worked. They learned how to take "book learning" and apply it practically. They learned how to learn.

Gradually I realized that following God really does make us the head and not the tail. We are never shortchanged. Real-life education was been the very *best* preparation my children could have received. They are now ready to learn and grow in service wherever God will call them.

I began this "impossible" writing assignment knowing that, just as God gave Bezaleel the needed talents to handcraft the furnishings for the wilderness tabernacle (Exodus 31:1–5), He would give me the help I needed to write about His guidance in our lives. I was finally ready to believe that God is able to complete what He calls us to start.

Our story is not the most amazing, sensational, or profound. It is simply a review of what God has done for our ordinary family as we chose to follow His extraordinary leading. Although the journey has been rough, we do not desire pity or praise. Our goal is to glorify, uplift, and honor the Lord. He has "authored" the story; I simply tried to put it on paper. We have blundered and made many mistakes along the way. Despite this, and maybe even because of it, we pray your faith can be strengthened, as ours has been, through the "ups and downs" of our experience. This story is not about the John Dysinger family, but about our God and His faithfulness.

Here we raise our Ebenezer!

Pam Dysinger
Williamsport, TN
October 2016

About This Book

Just a few words about the construction of this story. Most of the writing is mine, although John has done considerable editing and has expanded on some of the lessons we've learned. These insights are formatted as follows:

ABSOLUTE SURRENDER

Surrender is considered a bad word these days; it is associated with weakness and loss. But God's ways are not man's ways

In addition, there is much material excerpted from journals. My entries are as follows:

December 1992

Oh Lord, we thank You for new life! As this little child grows within me, I pray that I will grow in You. I want to pass from infancy to maturity in Christ. I know the task of

And John's:

April 17, 1991

Mark that date on the calendar as one of the top five in my life—for it was on this day I learned I was going to be a "Daddy!" . . . What a life-changing event! I'm sure

We encourage all to keep journals of God's faithful leading! Without our journals to prompt us, much of our story would have faded and been lost with the passing years.

Some names have been changed to protect the privacy of individuals, but the details remain as accurate as our memories and journals.

Dedication

To our precious children: Kirsten, Jonathan, Joshua, Zachariah, and Caleb. This grand adventure was for you! Thank you for the way you have handled the stern discipline of farm life. You could have resented God's leading, but you didn't. As you are reminded of His faithfulness in our past, we pray it will inspire you to continue serving the Lord our God with *all* your hearts. As God leads, lay all on the altar, be radical, be faithful, and know that He will never let you down!

We love you!
Mom and Dad

CHAPTER 1

The "Roller Coaster" Ride

WINTER 1987–FALL 1988

The silence of our tiny apartment was shattered by the loud ringing of the telephone. The caller's familiar voice belonged to Elder B. Months earlier, when John and I applied for a mission call to Nairobi, Kenya, Elder B had informed us that we needed experience, and preferably master's degrees, before we could seriously be considered for the call. Disappointed, we began to look for job opportunities here in the States. But now, to my utter amazement, I heard Elder B saying, "Mrs. Dysinger, the couple we hired for the job in Kenya has backed out . . . have you taken other jobs, or would you and John still be willing to consider the call?"

I could hardly believe my ears! I will forever remember the feeling of joy and peace that came after completely surrendering a heart's desire, and then, unexpectedly, receiving it back.

In May, 1987, John graduated with a degree in religious education from Southern College of Seventh-day Adventists in Collegedale, TN. Six weeks later, surrounded by family and friends, we joyfully began our married lives together. That fall we returned to college where I was finishing a degree in elementary education while John worked as the assistant chaplain.

Not long after our wedding, we began applying for overseas positions. We planned to go out as missionaries as soon as possible after my graduation. We looked forward to a "successful" life filled with work for the Lord. We thought we had it all together, and it seemed that others thought so too. Teachers and friends said things like, "The two of you won't have any problem landing a job!" and "It will be a lucky school that gets you guys."

With such praise ringing in our ears, we confidently applied for an open position at a boarding academy (private high school) in Kenya which served the children of missionaries from all over Africa. It quickly became clear that Maxwell Academy did not recognize what a "catch" we were. They were not interested in young upstarts like us. "Call us when you have some experience and maybe a master's degree" was the disappointing reply. We might be graduating from formal schooling, but we still had much to learn about humility, surrender, and waiting on God!

We began looking at boarding academies in the United States. Our first choice was an opening for a Bible teacher in the mountains of North Carolina. We sent out resumes and personally contacted the school. The response was becoming all too familiar: "Call us when you have some experience; when you're a little older . . ."

Undaunted, we sent out dozens of resumes to other boarding academies all over the United States, but the replies were all the same. *If they want experience, how was anyone to get it,* we wondered. Discouragement grew stronger every day. Graduation loomed ahead with no prospects of employment. Baffled by continued rejection, we prayed for understanding and for patience to wait on God for guidance.

We couldn't go overseas. No boarding academies wanted us. So we began looking at day academies and junior highs. Here we found school boards that were at least willing to consider us. John struggled with feelings of disappointment as he surrendered his dream of teaching at a boarding academy. What else could we do? In April, just three weeks before my graduation, we had appointments for two interviews. One was for an elementary school in the mountains of western Maryland, the other with a junior academy in upstate New York.

The interview in Maryland was first. It was a small, two-teacher school where I would teach grades 1–4 and John 5–8. The rural setting of the school and surrounding community was definitely what we were looking for. The school board won our hearts, and I guess we won theirs too, because before the interview was over, they offered us the job! We assured them we would pray about it and get back with them. As we drove on to New York, we talked excitedly and dreamed about all the things we could do with that little school. We loved the thought of working closely together. To my amazement, I saw my husband embracing the idea that this might be God's plan for us.

Upstate New York is a long drive from Tennessee, but the hours passed rapidly as we talked and analyzed what we were going through. What were we learning? Certainly surrender was the theme. As we arrived in Glens Falls, we were met by the school board chairman who took us out to lunch. Afterwards we drove up to the school and could see at a glance that this would be very different from that two-room school in Maryland. Walking through the cold, empty halls, we imagined the hustle and bustle of students filing in and out of classes. Yes, it was different, but this was much more in line with what John was trained to teach. Again we found favor in the eyes of the school board, and they offered jobs to both of us on the spot. Needing time to think and pray, we said we would get back to them within a week.

The discussion began as we closed the car doors—even before we got out of the school parking lot. For years John had been focused on working with high-school-age youth in a boarding academy setting. The New York school fit best with John's qualifications, yet, comparing the two openings before us, we both felt drawn to the position in Maryland. We analyzed the situation from every angle and went home planning to accept the first job offer. We simply wanted to be in God's will, and it seemed we had discovered it. Peace flooded our hearts, and excitement grew as we made plans for "our" little school.

Back at college, we took a few days to think, pray, and counsel with others before making our final decision. Once John was confident that Maryland was God's will, he made plans to call them on a Wednesday, ten days before graduation. For some unexplained reason, John didn't call that day. I was a bit disappointed and couldn't understand his delay.

On Thursday morning, before he had time to make the call, our phone rang. I could see from the expression on John's face that it was serious and seemed to relate to our job search. When he hung up, I was eager to know the details. "That was the boarding academy in North Carolina. They are wanting me to consider the school pastor and Bible teacher position!"

Unbelievable! What if John had made the call to Maryland yesterday? Or what if the North Carolina school had called tomorrow? We rejoiced that God was working on our behalf, stretching our faith, and opening doors at the very last minute. Everything was lining up beautifully. John was happy about the job. All disappointment about the Kenya job vanished as we basked in the sense of God's leading. It would have been nice to work overseas, but now we were perfectly content with the prospects of a boarding academy here in the States. Life was good! We changed mental gears again and started making plans for the move east . . . until the very next day. On Friday, the phone rang again. Would we still be interested in that position in Kenya?

One week before my graduation weekend, we were thrilled to accept a six-year teaching position at Maxwell Adventist Academy thirty minutes outside of Nairobi, Kenya. We had learned many amazing lessons, and thankfulness filled our hearts that the roller coaster ride was over—or so we thought!

ABSOLUTE SURRENDER

Surrender is considered a bad word these days; it is associated with weakness and loss. But God's ways are not man's ways (Isaiah 55:8, 9). Over and over again we have seen that our total surrender sets God free to work in powerful ways.

You've probably heard analogies comparing the Christian life to driving a car. As followers of Christ, we are supposed to let Him be in the driver's seat. The problem is, we like to be in control! Too often we grab the steering wheel and say, "No, that's not the way. We need to go this way." Inevitably when we do this, we end up in the ditch!

Absolute surrender is sitting still in the passenger's seat, completely trusting Christ to steer us safely home. Christ Himself set the example in the Garden of Gethsemane when He said to His Father, "Not my will but thine be done" (Luke 22:42).

In our experience, this complete surrender brings with it a peace and joy that is incomparable to anything this world can offer. Amazingly, after all the trials and "detours," we often end up right where we were wanting to go in the first place. But by then we have the confident assurance that it is His plan, and not just our own.

Two days after graduation, the moving van arrived to collect our meager belongings. We went on salary, started a tour to say our goodbyes to family, and worked through the many details related to moving overseas. We were in a daze as things came together in such rapid succession. Everything that is, except our work permits. Week after week, there was no change. For some unknown reason, the Kenyan government was not granting us permits. We prayed earnestly about this problem. Without the permits we could not go to Kenya. As we prayed, we also learned more about trust. In faith, we believed the documents would come through at the last possible minute, just as the job had. The summer of preparation flew by. Our belongings were crated and sitting in a Washington, D.C. warehouse. July was spent in Michigan at Mission Institute for orientation and training. Our goodbyes had been said and everything was in readiness.

August found us anxiously waiting. Then we received another call. It was the now-familiar voice of Elder B. "John, I have some bad news for you: . . . [still] no work permits . . . not sure why we can't secure them. . . . [I'm] forced to cancel your call to Kenya!"

We were devastated! Our hopes and dreams were dashed. What now? What do two jobless teachers do at the end of August? No school is looking for teachers that late in the year! We prayed, and the Lord was faithful to draw near, giving comfort, hope, and courage to our faint hearts. With a measure of peace restored, we began to look prayerfully at our remaining options. Very quickly the scope narrowed. We felt that the Lord was leading us to Michigan, where John would attend Andrews University and begin a master's degree program.

Finding a little apartment on campus, we unpacked our suitcases. What a relief it was to settle down after four months of upheaval! My nesting instincts kicked in. Our belongings were still in a warehouse in Washington, D.C. so I hunted for the basics at thrift stores. Disappointment over the events of the last few months subsided. *We don't really have to understand,* I told myself, *just trust the Lord.*

Job hunting was the next hurdle. The results of our earlier attempts left us without much courage. We ended up at a temporary job agency and were assigned to work at a Whirlpool factory. John's job was constructing cardboard boxes. Mine was to grab a motor from a conveyor belt, bubble wrap it, shove it into a box that seemed entirely too small, and get it back onto the belt before the next motor arrived. My fingers were soon raw and bleeding. Band-Aids provided momentary comfort, but they caught on the edges of the box and slowed me down.

Self-pity took up residence in my soul. *To think I went to school for sixteen years to do this! How humiliating! What would my friends think?* We felt completely out of place with the other workers. I am ashamed to say we did not focus on being a blessing to anybody. We nursed our wounds and plodded on in misery. At noon, we avoided the smoky lunchroom and retreated to the sunshine. There we would commiserate with each other, trying to make sense out of what seemed like pure confusion. Through it all, the Lord was calling us to a new level of surrender. We did try to answer that call.

School was about to start. Our finances did not look promising. Discouragement was tangible. *Lord, why have You taken us over this twisted trail?*

Close friends who lived nearby were the one bright spot in this troubled time. We enjoyed reconnecting as married couples. But even that joy could not mask the pain of being back in school instead of teaching. Our hearts were in Kenya, where the school year was already underway. We often thought of Tom and Nancy, a young couple we'd met at Mission Institute. They were in Kenya, working as boy's dean and elementary teacher. We wondered how they were adjusting. But what we really wondered was why *they* were in Kenya, and *we* were at the Whirlpool factory in Michigan! *Why?*

The morning of registration, John headed to the University. I was glad to stay "home." It felt good to settle in. Emotionally exhausted, I felt that it didn't matter where I was, as long as I could set up my home. We had finally accepted the graduate school idea, figured out the finances, and looked forward to being with our friends. The Whirlpool job, though, was more than I could bear, so I applied to work in the public school system as a substitute teacher. John arrived home from registering, and with excitement in his voice he began telling me about his classes, his teachers, and his advisor. Life was looking up. We were at peace . . . but then the phone rang.

Elder B's voice was yet again on the other end. "John, you're not going to believe this, but we have just secured your work permits. . . . Can you still come?" Inside I wanted to scream, *NO! I have had enough of this! I'm finally unpacked and I do not want to pack it all back up! They have missed their chance for us.* Emotions that I thought I'd already dealt with came tumbling out in a torrent of tears. I didn't want to go anymore! Maxwell Academy was already six weeks into the school year. I was sick and tired of being unsettled.

Overwhelmed, we went to our knees. "Father, what is *Your* will in this matter? What would *You* have us to do?" In a very short time, we both knew the answer. The University was willing to refund books and tuition. Once again we were packing. It wasn't long before I was praising God for the multitude of lessons He was teaching us. Looking back, we see God's hand in it all—stretching our faith and teaching total surrender to Him. Trials open our eyes to life's true richness. At the time, it can be difficult to see the blessing, but God knows how to use every experience for our good.

Finally, we were off to Kenya! From the start, we somehow knew that we were not being called to make a career of overseas missions. We believed that God was going to use this mission experience to prepare us for our real "mission field" back in the States. In the end, working with the children of missionaries had a profound effect on our lives—changing our outlook and perspective. God knew better than we did how much we would need to learn from those years of mission service. But for now, we were just thrilled to be stepping off the roller coaster!

CHAPTER 2

The Kenya Years

FALL 1988–SPRING 1994

═══════════════ **September 30, 1988** ═══════════════

Well, here I am looking down on the "Dark Continent" as it is touched with the very first light of dawn. . . . As the sun signals the beginning of a new day, I can't help but see it as symbolic of what's dawning in Pam's and my lives.

Below us—somewhere still shrouded in darkness—lies our new life. . . . I can't help but feel a little scared as I think about the job ahead and the many unknowns. . . . Six years—that's an awfully long time! What will I be like in six years? Six years means kids and over 30 years of age! Dear God, may we learn to take just one day at a time.

Farewells are always difficult. The thought of leaving our families for two whole years (between furloughs) was overwhelming! Yet the excitement of this new adventure pushed those feelings aside. The plane descended in preparation for landing. Flying in low over a Nairobi game park, we could see herds of gazelle grazing on the African savannah. What wild adventures awaited us in this new, Kenyan chapter of our lives?

Adrenaline made it hard to wait for our turn to disembark. At the baggage claim we piled our ten 70-pound boxes onto two carts and maneuvered clumsily through the airport. We could hardly push the load, let alone see over or around the boxes. Other travelers with their tourist-sized suitcases moved so easily, so casually through the lines to the waiting customs clerks, and quickly passed through.

As our turn approached, our eyes scanned the counters, praying for the kindest officer. Instead, a stern looking man called us forward. Bracing ourselves, we gave our buggies a "heave-ho," hoping we would not look too strained under the weight. The officer watched with wonder as we made this valiant effort.

"What's in all those boxes?" "our" customs official barked.

"Just personal belongings," was our quick reply. We explained that we were moving to Nairobi to work at a school for missionaries' children. We hoped that the officer could see that this explanation justified the large box that obviously contained a computer.

"Is that a computer?"

"Yes, sir. Here is our documentation to prove that we paid less than five thousand dollars—"

"You can't bring that in!"

"Sir, we were told—"

"I don't care what you were told." He didn't even look at our paperwork. Pen in hand, he scrawled, "57,000 shillings (approximately $2,000 US dollars) duty" on our computer box. We silently prayed, trying every reasonable argument we could think of, but there was no budging this man! Paying this exorbitant fee was totally out of the question, so the computer was impounded with the hope we would eventually cooperate with their system. (After many trips to the airport and haggling with the officers we finally secured it for a "meager" $500.) This was the first of many disturbing experiences with a corrupt and dishonest system of "negotiations."

Customs behind us, we started to process the fact that our feet now stood on African soil. This was our home for the next six years! Six years seemed to be a very long time, especially for me. Up to that time, I had never lived anywhere for more than three and a half years!

Scanning the waiting crowd, we finally saw a man holding a sign with our names on it. The school principal, accompanied by the bus driver, greeted us warmly and led us to a small, white bus where we loaded all those 70-pound boxes. As we moved out of the airport parking lot and onto the African roads, I was met with my next bit of culture shock. Growing up in the United States left me totally unprepared for the crowded, pot-hole-riddled roads. We felt like kernels of popcorn bouncing around in the bus. And then there was the dust. Rusty-red grime poured through the windows covering everything with a gritty film. Swerving left and right, the driver dodged potholes while our stomachs worked hard to keep down the airline breakfast we had eaten. Thirty minutes later, the very dusty bus filled with dusty boxes and dusty people arrived at its destination.

For many years, Maxwell Academy operated in the suburbs of Nairobi. As the city grew, its encroachment and influence on the students became a mounting concern. Two years before our arrival, a piece of land was purchased, and the school moved to a stunning setting at the base of the Ngong Hills. Here the giraffe and gazelle freely roamed the campus and the students were surrounded by the sights of nature.

Because the school was still under construction, we were informed that we would live, "for the first year or two," in a prefabricated metal box measuring just seven hundred square feet. On the bus ride we learned that Tom and Nancy, the young couple we had met at Mission Institute, were living in "our" house. The plan was that we would share that tiny house until their apartment in the boys' dormitory was completed. This completion was going to happen "in a couple of weeks."

Mercifully, we did not realize that this was our introduction to African time. "African time" refers to the relaxed attitude towards scheduled appointments as compared to the more clock-bound pace of daily life in Western countries. It is good that we did not know that our "couple of weeks" of house sharing would be a couple of months, and the "year or two" in the prefab house would actually turn into six years.

Our first new day in Kenya was the Sabbath. As the morning sun streamed through the windows of our metal box home, we crawled groggily out of bed. We were determined to jump right into our new life even though the time zone was seven hours ahead of our biological clocks. Heading for the shower we discovered that there was no water. To make matters worse, the electricity was off! The principal's house had water, we were told. We could have a cold shower there. But that meant a long, self-conscious walk all the way across the middle of campus, right in front of the boys' and girls' dormitories! We felt many curious eyes peering out the windows, sizing up the disheveled young Bible teacher and his wife as they hurried by with heads lowered, towels and clean clothes in hand. We were definitely out of our comfort zone now. At the principle's home we took short, invigorating showers. Of course, there would be no blow dryer or curling iron without electricity. We faced introductions to our new students "as is." Welcome "home"!

This new beginning got even better when we arrived at church and were given the "opportunity" to do special music. What ever made them think of that? Too foggy from jet-lag to think clearly, we couldn't muster up the good sense to just say no. John had the bright idea that we would just teach them a new song. After all, that's why we were here! To teach them new things!

Surprise! The students already knew "Jesus is the Answer"! Well, anyway, we could sing it together, right? Wrong. It took only a few discordant notes to reach the painful conclusion that the young people were enthusiastically singing our words, but to a completely unfamiliar tune. Ugh! Somehow we stumbled through, and slunk back to our seats. My bright red face advertised my embarrassment. We were off to a *great* start!

We hit the Kenyan ground running. On Monday morning, John started teaching—ready or not! I struggled with discouragement because I was just assigned odd jobs. This was almost as bad as Whirlpool! I had not yet learned that any work needing to be done is worth doing with all your might. I found myself cooking in the cafeteria and cataloging books in what was going to be the school library. The most gratifying job they assigned to me was teaching social studies at the small elementary school on campus.

We crawled through each never-ending day of our first few months in Kenya under the overwhelming realization that a six-year commitment was something akin to eternity. Daily we struggled with anxious feelings. John lay awake at night, drenched in cold sweats. The immensity of his responsibilities as spiritual leader of the school weighed heavily upon him. Through it all, we clung to the memories of God's miraculous leading in the past. We chose to trust that He would not forsake us, even though we were so far from everything familiar. We were determined to learn whatever lessons our heavenly Father chose to teach us on this foreign soil.

For the next six years we learned about adaptability. John taught three Bible classes, preached twice a month, led all the weekend spiritual activities, and spent two evenings a week counseling in the dormitories. At various times he was also the assistant dean, health and PE teacher, and head of the landscaping crew. I too received a variety of assignments, but mainly taught in the small, one-room elementary school. Nancy, who had been hired as teacher, got pregnant that first year, so I was asked to teach full-time the second year. Many stories could be told about our years in Kenya. After the initial culture shock and awkwardness, we made many friends—not only with staff and students, but with the surrounding community. The Lord abundantly blessed our ministry to the students. We learned many, many lessons that enriched our lives. But the focus of this book is on how God led us into farming, so we will stick mainly with events that directly affected our eventual calling to agricultural pursuits.

=============================== *April 17, 1991* ===============================

Mark that date on the calendar as one of the top five in my life—for it was on this day I learned I was going to be a "Daddy!" . . . What a life-changing event! I'm sure this will be the beginning of many such events in the next few months and years! . . . May I never take this responsibility lightly.

On December 18, 1991, Kirsten Noelle Dysinger joined our family. It was a rather traumatic birth. There was no fetal monitoring. The baby was in distress. The short umbilical cord was wrapped around her neck twice. She had to be vacuum extracted. We know the protecting hand of God was on Kirsten's life from the beginning.

A petite little girl, Kirsten was a bright-eyed bundle of energy! We were awestruck at the brilliance of the Master Designer who fashioned her tiny fingers and toes. Basking in the new-found depths of love and awareness that came into our lives as we were transformed into parents, we thoroughly enjoyed those first few days with our precious daughter.

Ten days after Kirsten's birth, my mother made the long trip to join us in our celebration. Having her there to enter into our joy and help us during that time of adjustment was another quantum leap in personal perspective. I saw my mother differently now. After experiencing the miracle of giving birth, I could now imagine how she had felt while carrying me in her womb, and then holding me for the first time. Our relationship moved to a more intimate level, and I was so thankful she was with us.

John and I were committed to doing everything we could to raise Kirsten in the best possible way. We were abundantly conscientious. We took everything seriously. Our daughter was such a source of pride and pleasure that the joy shone on our faces. We loved parenting so much that on December 8, 1992, just ten days before Kirsten's first birthday, I left a little green sticky note on John's computer that said, "Pregnancy test positive."

December 1992

Oh Lord, we thank You for new life! As this little child grows within me, I pray that I will grow in You. I want to pass from infancy to maturity in Christ. I know the task of raising children is difficult. I pray you will teach me to put self aside, enabling me to be the mother I was created to be.

Our fifth school year in Kenya was half over when we discovered the joyful news that our second child was on the way. With one child, life had not changed very much. I continued teaching part time, and managed fairly normally. But with two babies under two years of age, something had to give. John and I both felt that I needed to put my attention and energy into our home and family. At the least, I needed to have a less demanding job at the school. But there were nagging questions.

How could I resign? Who would replace me? The school couldn't just go out and hire another teacher! There were huge expenses involved with moving someone overseas. The school only had so much money in its budget. I felt committed to my students and found it difficult to walk away from my job. One evening the parents of three of my students sat in our living room and asked us our thoughts about the upcoming school year. These true friends were not thinking of themselves or how my decision would impact their family. Instead they pointed me to the important role of motherhood and encouraged me to follow through with our convictions. I shared my struggle with the decision to resign.

"Pam, just trust the Lord," my friends encouraged me. It was a step of faith. Once I made the decision and turned in my resignation letter, perfect peace flooded my soul. As I trusted the Lord with the details, He worked it all out. Very quickly the school administration found a volunteer who gladly filled my position.

August 15, 1993, Jonathan Louis added a new dimension to our family. Weighing a pound and a half more than his sister, he seemed extra plump and healthy. Everything went well the first week. We adjusted quickly to life as a family of four. John's mother, accompanied by Katie, an eleven-year-old great niece, came to help us this time. We had no idea at the time how much we would need her!

A week after Jonathan was born, everything started unraveling. Kirsten came down with a high fever. Next, Katie became ill. After that, I got the fever. John was soon sick, and finally Jonathan's temperature began to go up. The evening of Jonathan's eleventh day of life, the school nurse, who had been monitoring our illness, encouraged us to take Jonathan to the emergency room. The nurse advised me to stay home and rest, believing that John and his mother would simply take him in for a quick checkup. I felt so miserable that I agreed to this plan and went to bed.

At midnight my mother-in-law returned without John and Jonathan! The doctors had not come to a clear diagnosis and wanted to keep the baby for more testing. Now I wished I had gone with them. How could I sleep knowing that my sick husband and baby were lying in an African hospital? Anxious and distressed, I took a hot shower and tried to relax. Dropping to my knees by my bed, I asked the Lord to take away my anxious feelings and give me His peace. When I crawled back under my lonely covers, peace came, and so did sleep.

The next morning, I left Kirsten with my friend Nancy and headed for the hospital. In a daze, I walked down the hall to Jonathan's room. There, in a little incubator, lay my precious baby boy. He looked so perfectly strong and healthy. How could he be so sick? On a cot next to the incubator slept John, the faithful father, flushed with fever. It all felt like a bad dream!

Test after test revealed nothing definitive for any of us. They ruled out malaria, typhoid fever, meningitis, and other terrible diseases, but no diagnosis was ever made for John or me. Jonathan was finally diagnosed with "neonatal sepsis"—a general term for any blood infection that occurs in an infant younger than ninety days old. A little research informed us that neonatal sepsis is a leading cause of infant death. Our hearts were constantly lifted up in prayer for our son. It was the most intense call to surrender we had yet experienced.

Five days later, Jonathan was released from the hospital. We soon realized he was still not well. Of course, we were not strong either, and by this time my mother-in-law was gone. We struggled to manage on our own.

School was back in session, and even though John was still sick he had responsibilities. Of course there were all the regular rigors of the school year. In addition, there was a special commitment weekend for the new students. This weekend was an effort to lead the young people into a deeper relationship with Christ before the new school term. God miraculously blessed us with His strength and Spirit. Many lives were recommitted to Him. In spite of all the added stress, John and I slowly gained strength. Jonathan, on the other hand, continued to struggle. Every afternoon, his fever would spike in spite of our best efforts to keep him cool. Again and again I took my baby to the doctor who gave him an injection. The fever would drop, and we would go back home until the next day. Exhaustion set in as I struggled to manage the home while John tried to keep up with his work for the school.

At last the fevers began to recede and in time the Lord gave Jonathan a complete and total recovery. Through this trial we learned the important lesson that we are only stewards of our children. They belong to the Lord and we are to trust their lives into His hands. It was amazing how God's peace replaced my desperate struggling when I chose to remember that "my" children are, in reality, His children.

The gift of parenthood changed our whole outlook on life. Examining ourselves, we saw that the defects in our own characters must be overcome if we wanted to lead our children in the right way. We started observing our students more closely. The Bible condemns judging, but we are told that we may learn a lot from being fruit inspectors (see Matthew 7:20). When we recognized excellent "fruit" in the life of a student, we tried to learn more about his or her family. Our desire was to know what other parents had done to encourage these good character traits in their children.

I remember one such "interview" with two brothers. Their mother had accompanied them to school their first year, helped them to enroll, and got them settled in. That was very unusual! We invited the boys for dinner and picked their brains about how they had been raised. The conversation started slowly because I'm sure they had never thought about these things from a young parent's perspective. As they warmed up to the subject, memories of a loving, Christian home brought forth loads of data for our poll. One thing I remember them saying is that they talked to their parents about everything. I thought that was quite unusual. The boys smiled as they recounted how they would pile onto their parents' bed and talk for hours. On school breaks they did things as a family: played games, took vacations, had family worship, ministered with their parents. They had great memories of Mom making their favorite foods. Their parents succeeded at creating an environment where the whole family just enjoyed being together.

Unfortunately, there were not a lot of young people bearing the kind of fruit we were looking for. Many troubled students shared deep pain and anger against their parents. Some were bitter against the church for keeping the parents so busy "serving the Lord" that they had no significant time and energy for their own youngsters. When the young people returned to school from vacations, we often asked them what they did at home. "We watched movies," was the standard answer. Probing deeper didn't make things sound any better. In our hearts we cried, *What! No family time? No vacation? No playing together? No making memories?* It was heart breaking! John's two nights a week in the dorms could not satisfy the counseling needs. Far too many of these young people were hurting. The parents were out saving the "heathen" but losing their own precious flock. We do not believe God asks His servants to make this kind of sacrifice. We prayed for wisdom to understand what servanthood should look like in the context of a family.

We were dealing with youngsters from eighteen or twenty different nationalities. No matter what culture parents come from, if they do not work, play, and worship with their children, they are losing opportunities to create and enrich the bonds that should exist between parents and children. We believe the results of our "fruit inspection" would be about the same if we had been teaching in the United States. The family structure is crumbling everywhere and everyone suffers from the results.

John's involvement with counseling took him from our home more evenings than it should have. After one unusually heavy day, I was worn out with domestic responsibilities. *"At times I feel like a single parent,"* I wrote home. John's time was consumed with teaching, preaching, spiritual activities, and counseling. Often there was precious little left for the children and me. One evening, after he stayed in the dorm longer than expected, I sat him down and said, "John, if something doesn't change, someday someone else is going to be counseling your children."

Looking back, I know God put those words in my mouth, because they cut like a knife to my husband's heart and gave him the determination to seek change.

Sitting on the discipline committee was another part of John's pastoral work. The issues they dealt with covered the whole range of teenage problems. Some of the issues were so shocking I could never bring myself to write them down! Even now I can hardly believe some of the things that went to the discipline committee. I shudder to think of the many more that were never uncovered. One young man committed suicide, apparently to keep from facing his father with his misdemeanor. Another missionary kid told John, "If my dad is in heaven, I don't want to be there." Words like these definitely affected our thinking! We began asking ourselves, "How is it going to be any different for us?"

To begin with, we prayed. We prayed a lot. We determined that we were going to be involved in our children's lives. We tried to understand how to be more connected. We wondered if that was enough. Was it possible to produce the "fruit" we desired in our family while remaining in a boarding school setting?

By the spring of 1994, just three months before we were scheduled to return permanently to the United States, we were suffering from burnout. For spring break we traveled to Tanzania, where we spent ten relaxing days with John's brother, Edwin, and his family. They lived on a five-thousand-acre farm where they were involved in community development. Here life was much slower and simpler. They lived without electricity. "Running water" was acquired by running to the stream with a bucket.

The basic home-maker's tasks of cooking and washing clothes consumed my days. I dropped into bed exhausted after each day's labor while John was exhilarated by this life of hard work. Standing under the stars one night, waiting our turn for the outhouse, John said, "Honey, this is the way life was meant to be!" I wasn't so sure about that. I was working hard to keep two little ones out of the dirt, helping with food preparation, doing dishes in cold water, sorting filthy grains and legumes, washing clothes and dirty diapers on a washboard . . . I was definitely not convinced that this was "the way life was meant to be."

Despite the increased workload it took just to stay alive and clean, our time with Edwin, Jennifer, Evie, Caroline, and Paul did provide us with the change of pace and surroundings we needed. We spent our evenings sitting together in the lamplight, listening to sermon tapes that encouraged us to a deeper, more serious relationship with Christ. The focus was on abiding in Christ and how we can live a victorious Christian life. That was exactly what we were longing for! We were a bit disillusioned with the "normal" Christian life. We were looking for alternatives. Here we listened to the testimony of a family who had simply made the decision to pull out of the rat-race that we euphemistically call the "American Dream." They went in search of God, and they found Him!

We were energized! We didn't have to be victims of circumstance; we *could* take charge of our lives. The simplicity of Edwin and Jennifer's life, combined with the practical messages we were listening to empowered us! Sitting in that lamp-lit room, surrounded by the sounds of the African night, we were emboldened to change. It was clear to us that this change had to start in the home circle. So on our last night in Tanzania, with millions of stars in the African sky as our witness, we committed to do *anything* God led us to for the saving of our family. There would be no cost too high! Unsure of what we had committed to, we returned to Kenya to complete our last few weeks of school.

~ JERUSALEM FIRST ~

Our experience working with missionary's children taught us the value of the "Jerusalem First" principle.

In Mark 16:15 Christ gave the disciples (and us) the great commission. He said, "go ye into all the world, and preach the gospel to every creature." Many go out with great fervor to convert the "heathen" while forgetting the rest of Christ's instruction. In Luke 24:47–49, He added that the disciples were to begin in Jerusalem and to wait there until He sent the Holy Spirit to empower them. In Acts 1:8 He clarifies that after they received the Holy Spirit, they were to witness in Jerusalem, then Judea, then Samaria, then to the "uttermost part of the earth."

Throw a rock into a pond and the ripples move outward in ever widening circles. So the witness and influence of our lives goes out to the world around us. If we are faithful, that testimony and influence will bless many. However, our calling starts in "Jerusalem." We see this "Jerusalem" as the home circle. If our Christianity is not transforming our own families, then we have absolutely nothing to share with the world. What people really want and need is the influence of a practical Christianity that changes our own lives where the rubber meets the road.

In our zeal to evangelize the world, we often fail to realize that godly families have a more powerful witness than the greatest sermons ever preached. "Jerusalem first" is not selfish isolationism; it's actually mobilizing the greatest evangelistic force in the world!

After leaving Edwin's family, we returned to our work in Kenya with one very important question on our minds. "What next?" We prayed. We pursued one job possibility after another. We wondered how the Lord was going to lead us to a better situation for our family. It was a time of real soul searching.

On our next weekend off we went to a nearby guest house and pored over the Bible for guidance about life-work and parenting. Through God's Word we began to see a beautiful picture of what families are intended to be. It is not a picture of the fractured modern family. It is a picture of parents who train their children in the ways of the Lord from the moment they rise in the morning to the time they lie down at night (Deuteronomy 6:7).

How could any parents anywhere manage to do that while living today's modern lifestyle? We found that Paul charged the Thessalonians to lead a quiet life and work with their hands (1 Thessalonians 6:7). That was a new thought to us! What, exactly, did following Paul's counsel look like for us? We tucked our study into the back of our minds and continued to pray. While we still had no clear direction, we did have the assurance that God would make His path clear to us in His time.

Changes in Perspective

Soon after returning from our spring break in Tanzania we were swept up again in the whirlwind of school activities. A college recruiter from the United States came to do a week of prayer. The recruiter and his wife of twenty-five years looked forward to adding a safari to this exotic trip to Africa. I was the guest-house hostess, so I often had opportunity to visit with this couple.

While our Week of Prayer speaker and his wife occupied the guest house, another guest arrived on campus. He was a single man, and he too needed a place to stay for a couple of nights. He had a bad back, so I couldn't just put him on the floor somewhere. He needed a bed, and the only bed I had left was the one in the second bedroom in the guest house. I innocently asked the recruiter's wife if they would mind letting this man use the smaller bedroom of the guest house. To my amazement, that simple request opened a flood gate of frustration. Mrs. Recruiter spewed out a terrible torrent of pent-up feelings and emotions that left me feeling half drowned. No, they did *not* want this man to intrude on their long-looked-forward-to holiday. They had sacrificed greatly to keep their children in private Christian schools. They had lived with no vacations, old clothes, old cars, old furniture. Their children were utterly unappreciative of their many sacrifices. Life was disappointing and unfair. They were looking forward to this time alone and did not want to share the guest house with anyone.

Once I caught my breath, I could not fault the couple. Maybe I shouldn't have asked for such a favor, but if I hadn't, I would not have been given such an educational glimpse into the lives of two very un-happy "servants of the Lord." I was reminded that the tapestry of life can look beautiful to the casual observer, but a little stress reveals the weakness of the fabric.

Our unexpected guest slept gratefully on an air mattress on our living room floor, unaware of the storm his presence had precipitated. We managed just fine.

During the recruiter couple's stay, we had other opportunities to visit. In my zeal over our new ideas on our future and the raising of our children, I shared some thoughts about a simpler, more balanced life. I pictured a life in which raising our children for the Lord would be paramount. To Mrs. Recruiter's way of thinking, these were pipe dreams. She considered our ideas and goals to be unrealistic. In her desire to give my youthful idealism a reality check, she spoke words that I will never forget. "Pam, it will be no different for you than it's been for me. Your husband will climb the denominational ladder just like mine has." Hastily I wrapped up the conversation. My mind reeled with the ramifications of her words and my heart screamed, *No! Lord, please, not like their life, . . . I want it to be different!*

The recruiter's wife was one more link in God's chain of events de-signed to change the course of our lives! Her words put skin on things we had observed at a distance. So many student families whose children were older than ours were letting us observe the results of their career, parenting, and life choices by sending their children to "our" school. Mrs. Recruiter will never know how sorry I felt for her, and how per-sistently her words and her life confirmed the things the students were teaching us. Her visit to "our" guest-house has come to mind again and again through the years. It seems clear to me that she was not experi-encing the true joy God intended us to have in marriage, family, and the Christian walk. I came away from this experience determined, by God's grace, that this would *not* be our testimony.

The hustle and bustle of change took over our lives after the Week of Prayer. After six eventful years, it was time to return permanently to the States. We still had to wrap up the school year—a daunting task in itself. The job of selling household belongings, packing, and selling our vehicle added another burden of work and weariness.

Graduation weekend brought mixed emotions. Our sixth class of seniors walked down the aisle and collected their diplomas. This was *our* class. We had been their class sponsors since they were in seventh grade! Of course there were not many who had been at the school since seventh grade, but there were many who had been there for four years. Graduations are always an emotional time and we were definitely feeling it this year! One looks with a kind of parental love at the young people who came onto campus as awkward early teens. Four years later they leave, very much more confident, and hopefully having developed talents and skills that prepare them for the next step in life. John had nurtured and mentored and done all he knew how to do for them. Always he sought to inspire them to give their hearts to the Lord. We wanted them to be truly successful.

In spite of the nostalgia, and in spite of some sadness, there was a great sense of emancipation. We were going HOME! We might be going to a place we had never been before, but that mattered not a bit. It would be in the States. It would be home in a sense that we had not experienced for the last six years.

May 29, 1994

John preached his last sermon and had his last baptism. It was a high day, full of sadness and relief. Like Joshua of old, John challenged the students to join him in saying, "As for me and my house, we will serve the Lord." All I could do was cry and cry. It has been so busy and hectic. Sometimes I felt like a single mother with John so busy. I have not been the kind, consistent, patient mother I want to be. Lord, I feel so far from You. I don't understand where You're leading our future. Do we go to Andrews for John's master's degree, or to the little one-room Centerville school near John's parents? How do we decide? You know. What would be best for our little family?

June 12, 1994

Goodbye to Kenya! Friday evening we sold our car, then watched the sun setting behind the Ngong Hills as it drove away. We spent Sabbath with our dear Masai friends who live on the hill behind the school. A few last things went into our boxes, and then we were off to the airport.

That evening we sat on the floor of our "tin hut" for the last time, feverishly packing boxes. We reminisced about the six years that had gone by so slowly, and yet so fast. Six years was long enough to cultivate deep friendships. Not only had we grown to love the staff families, but also the students and many people from the surrounding community. These friends had enriched our lives and filled them with meaning. Goodbyes were not easy; we already missed each one. We could finally laugh over the mortifying experiences of our first weekend in Kenya. Irregular electricity was no problem now; hanging out laundry and dusty, pothole-filled roads were normal. At the beginning, six years seemed like eternity, but suddenly they were gone. We had grown in every way! Wherever the Lord would lead us, the lessons learned in Kenya would influence the rest of our lives.

CHAPTER 3

Andrews to Self-employment

SPRING 1994—SUMMER 1997

◇◇◇◇◇◇◇◇◇◇◇◇◇◇◇◇◇◇◇◇◇◇◇◇◇◇◇◇◇◇◇◇◇ ***June 14, 1994*** ◇◇◇◇◇◇◇◇◇◇◇◇◇◇◇◇◇◇◇◇◇◇◇◇◇◇◇◇◇◇◇◇◇

We're going to Andrews University, . . . trusting it's God's plan. . . .We've been
home two days and I keep having to remind myself that we're here to stay, it feels
so good!

Our years in Kenya definitely took a toll on our family. The pressure
of the work and the long hours stressed our marriage, our children, and
our relationship with the Lord. Although Kirsten and Jonathan were very
young when we returned to the States, they had still been affected by the
stress in our lives. We needed time for our family to reconnect and heal.

The decision to go to Andrews was not easy. We struggled with this
choice until the end of May, longing for some clear evidence that this
was, indeed, God's will. Looking back, we still wonder whether it was
the right decision. Not only did it take a large part of our savings, but
John certainly did not need a master's in educational psychology to be
a farmer! There were blessings that came from our decision. We had
much needed time to rest and recuperate. Our six years at Maxwell laid

26

the foundation for our future. Perhaps the "cement" in that foundation needed to "cure"—to settle, to solidify.

During John's school days, he spent evenings and weekends playing with the children. We often piled both of them into the wagon and pulled it to a nearby playground. It was one of our favorite ways to spend family time. I reveled in the fact that I was responsible for my own children, and no others. We were no longer off duty once a month. We were off every weekend! No discipline committee, no counseling in the dorms, no supervisory duties! I felt like a caged bird set free. At Andrews, very few people knew us. We had no church responsibilities. John attended all of his classes and did very well, but he was never a slave to his studies. Life was simple, happy, and fulfilling. Those ten months in Michigan were like an oasis in our lives, and we praised the Lord for allowing us this "sabbatical."

Much of our new-found freedom was spent on seeking to know the Lord better. We dug deeper into God's Word, mining for hidden treasures that would teach us God's goals for our lives. We began to understand more about God's plan for families. We prayed for wisdom to take the principles we learned and apply them appropriately to our situation. We reflected on and analyzed the lessons we had learned from teaching high-schoolers. We came to believe that we should work with younger children in order to have a more lasting impact on their character development. Hopefully such work would impact the families as well. Sooner than we wished, we were again facing an unknown future. How we did pray for God's clear guidance!

A little church school in Centerville, Tennessee had offered us a job a year earlier. That school was again looking for a teacher. Maybe we should have wondered why they were looking for their third teacher in three years, but we didn't. Our name went on their list of possibilities and we hoped that this job would be offered to us. Our hopes dimmed when we heard about a "Mrs. K" whose situation seemed to indicate that she should get the job. John began preparing his resume while God continued to work out *His* plan. For reasons that remain a mystery to us, "Mrs. K" did not get the job. Someone told us she didn't want it. We were overjoyed to accept a call to Centerville!

On May 29, 1995, John moved the children and me to his parents' farm, twenty-five minutes from the Centerville school. Then he returned to Andrews for six weeks to finish up his degree.

We hated the separation! In our twenty-nine years of marriage this six-week stretch remains the longest we have ever been apart. Six weeks was just too long to go without seeing each other. Friends in Louisville, Kentucky generously offered their home to us while they were away. It wasn't exactly half way between Centerville and Berrien Springs, but we accepted the offer and enjoyed a blissful weekend of fun and family fellowship. We worshipped together, played together, and relaxed together. The most exciting part of that weekend came in the form of a wonderful surprise.

Sabbath, June 25, 1995

I'm pregnant! I'm thrilled and fearful. A mother of three. THREE! Lord, thank you for Your leading and the strength I know You will give!

One year earlier we had suffered the heartache of a miscarriage, so we decided to keep our happy news to ourselves for a few more weeks. With happy hearts the children and I returned to Tennessee while John went back to Andrews and finished his course work.

Hunting for the "perfect" country property

Back in the summer of 1992, John and I came home on furlough from Kenya. We proudly introduced our little daughter to John's parents and they proudly showed off their retirement property in Tennessee. John and his brothers playfully bantered with their parents about where on their beautiful 190-acre piece of land each one would build his house. Of course, it was all in good fun. Nobody took it seriously because we were living in Kenya, one brother lived in Tanzania, and one in Guam. John's sister was settled in Maryland.

Being the realist in the family, I pulled John aside and suggested to him that he should not lead his parents on. "We'll never live here," I assured him emphatically. "What would we do for a living way out here in the sticks?" Oh, how little I knew of God's leading!

In the spring of 1995 we found ourselves living on the farm, but only temporarily! We were committed to living closer to the church school. In April we had our job interview, and we found the "perfect" property. It was just a mile from the church down a beautiful country lane—an old-fashioned farmhouse set on seventy beautiful, rolling acres. We were sure this was the place God had prepared for us. The price was right and we quickly made an offer.

To our dismay, we learned that another buyer, with a different realtor, had just signed a contract on "our" farm. Disappointed, we continued our search. A few weeks later the realtor contacted us and said that the new owners were going to sell the house with less acreage than originally specified. She wanted to know if we were still interested. The next four months were an emotional roller coaster. The new owner dangled the carrot in front of our faces repeatedly before snatching it away. They were going to sell. They were not going to sell. They were. They weren't.

Frustrated, disappointed, and confused, we finally gave up. It took me a long time to start considering my in-laws' farm as a long-term option. My independent nature kept me hunting for something else. In the end, I surrendered to the reality that God's plan was right under our feet. The Lord wanted us to build on the farm, right near to John's parents.

I did not yet realize the amazing blessing God had in store for our children. They were privileged to grow up on the same property with their grandparents. If only I had prayed seriously about that idea from the beginning, we could have saved ourselves months of longing and looking for that "perfect" country home. I needed to learn to wait upon the Lord. Unfortunately, I required still further education in the science of submission to God's plans.

November 1995 found us beginning construction on a small log cabin. I wanted to build on one of the secluded hills, but the Lord clearly led us to a beautiful spot in the valley. It was a serene setting bordered on two sides by creeks. The foundation and subfloor were in place when the logs arrived on December 18. It was Kirsten's fifth birthday.

Meanwhile, John had a rocky start at his new school. Teaching three active children in three different grades was a lot harder than it looked! John is very detail-oriented and focused. This made keeping up with a multi-grade classroom and its many lesson plans an overwhelming challenge. Everything about that first year was rough. We were building a house and doing much of the work ourselves. We lived with his parents. John had a new job. Besides all of this, I was pregnant! Needless to say, we were both totally overwhelmed!

On high-stress days, I learned to walk out of our basement apartment to the open air. Surrounded there by the quiet beauty of nature, my heart found peace. Life's difficulties somehow diminished to manageable proportions as I stood out there and breathed in God's fresh air. Country living was new to me and I began to love it.

February 21, 1996

Basking in the sunshine . . . skinning peanuts for butter. Kirsten and Jonathan riding bikes and playing Sabbath School. . . . We are all waiting. Waiting for Joshua's birth. The time is right. Thank You, Lord for the warmth of the sunshine.

Sabbath, February 24, 1996

8:45 a.m. Sent children off to church with Grandma and Grandpa.

9:30 a.m. Walked down the hill, enjoying the sunshine and gaining strength for the labor ahead.

2:16 p.m. Joshua is here!

On the Sabbath, God's memorial of creation, we saw in the most vivid way possible His creative power. Thank You, Father, for another healthy baby boy!

In spite of the joy, the stresses of life continued. The following journal entry gives a clue to our state of mind around the time of Joshua's birth.

February 28, 1996

The man I love is so discouraged it breaks my heart! Lord, why did You bring us here? We prayed long and hard for Your leading. We felt sure You were in this move. So why are things at school turning into a nightmare? Why, Lord? Please give us another dream, another purpose, another means of making a living. Show me how to support, honor, and encourage John as he grapples with this trial.

We were not meeting our goals. We questioned whether this was God's long-term plan for us. We hoped and prayed for a change. God did make a change, but that change was in us instead of in our situation. The school year ended better than it began, and John signed a contract for a second year.

Providential meeting

During the summer, John attended a teacher's convention where more than a thousand Adventist teachers gathered for inspiration and encouragement. Out of those thousand teachers, God wanted John to meet one in particular. The very first night of the convention, John introduced himself to a teacher who blurted out, "So you're the one who got the job I wanted!"

"What?" John was confused. This was the "Mrs. K" who, we thought, had turned down the job. "I heard you didn't want it!"

We never have figured out exactly how we ended up with the Centerville job, but it was certainly a part of God's pathway for us. At any rate, "Mrs. K" now had a face and a phone number. John tucked that information away for future reference.

Near the beginning of John's second school year at Centerville a new problem surfaced. Instead of three students in three grades there were now thirteen students in six grades. In a flash John saw the number of lesson plans change from eighteen to thirty per day. It was overwhelming.

To give John a break, I taught one day a week. This gave my husband some time with our children and the ability to work on the house. We were far too busy. It was as bad as boarding academy—or maybe even worse! At least at Maxwell we ate our meals together. Now John left the house in the morning just as the children got up. He did well to get home an hour before they went to bed. He just had enough time to have worship and tuck them into bed. Sundays were consumed with working on that beastly house project. We longed to get the house done so we could move on with life!

John is a man of many talents. These talents, however, do not include the management of a multi-grade classroom. Early in the second school year his job satisfaction hit an all-time low. He wasn't meeting his school goals, his family goals, his spiritual goals, or his personal goals. He didn't feel good about any area of his life. It all came to a head one night while I was at the school helping where I could, and providing moral support. Sitting amid the stacks of paper and books, John picked up the phone and called "Mrs. K." He explained that the Centerville teaching job was going to be available the following year and he hoped "she" would take it.

"Mrs. K" very kindly encouraged John to hang in there. "You'll feel better once the school year gets underway." He didn't! Despite the challenges, we did complete the school year. John did his best to reach the children. He gave them the education that is most valuable. Parents and students were oblivious to the fact that John struggled with a deep, heartfelt discontent. They were happy with their school and their teacher.

January 25, 1997

John sent his letter of resignation to the school board chairman.

January 26

John's letter will be read by the School Board today. The kerosene heater in the house has malfunctioned. Everything is covered with a thick layer of soot. I choose to thank You, Lord, for the trials. I sure wouldn't mind some help cleaning this up, though I won't ask anyone but You.

That sooty disaster set us weeks behind. The layer of black grime didn't just wipe off. The drywall had to be repainted; first with a sealant to keep the soot from showing through the paint, and then with two new coats of paint. We sanded and scrubbed the log walls. Three church members asked if they could help. With prayer for help from above, we accepted the offer and tackled the mess.

⬦⬦⬦⬦⬦⬦⬦⬦⬦⬦⬦⬦⬦ *Sabbath, February 1* ⬦⬦⬦⬦⬦⬦⬦⬦⬦⬦⬦⬦⬦

Today was our first time to see the school board chairman and other board members since they received the letter. Not much was said, but the pressure is on. . . . Lord, we believe You've led, but why does it have to be so hard?

Those were difficult days! We loved our church family and longed to take away the hurt and misunderstanding we had caused. Second guessing ourselves, we prayed over and over about our decision and the reasons for it. Seeking counsel was not easy but it was confirming. We didn't just ask those we thought would give us the answer we wanted to hear, but we did ask people who understood how to surrender all to God.

⬦⬦⬦⬦⬦⬦⬦⬦⬦⬦⬦⬦⬦ *February 2* ⬦⬦⬦⬦⬦⬦⬦⬦⬦⬦⬦⬦⬦

Restless night. A wise counselor asked a couple of pertinent questions:

1. If there were no hurt feelings and if extended family members were not involved, would we be indecisive about our decision?
2. What kind of family time do we need? Does the teaching job fit into that?

⬦⬦⬦⬦⬦⬦⬦⬦⬦⬦⬦⬦⬦ *February 3* ⬦⬦⬦⬦⬦⬦⬦⬦⬦⬦⬦⬦⬦

The board meets tomorrow evening. Word has leaked out. John received a letter from one of his students, pleading for him to reconsider. . . . We feel so torn. . . . This evening we were talking with the Lord when John just stopped. He said, "Honey, God has given me the answer! We can't turn back!" We went to bed at peace.

⬦⬦⬦⬦⬦⬦⬦⬦⬦⬦⬦⬦⬦ *February 4* ⬦⬦⬦⬦⬦⬦⬦⬦⬦⬦⬦⬦⬦

Some board members still wanted to change John's mind, but one of them spoke up and said, "If John feels convicted that this is what God is calling him to do, who are we to stand in the way?"

FAITH VS. PRESUMPTION

"Wasn't that presumptuous," some ask, "to quit your job when you had a family dependent on you?" In my mind the answer is plain: Faith is walking down the path God has clearly told you to follow. Presumption is walking down the path of your own choosing and still expecting God to bless you.

The garden provides an excellent example of the difference between faith and presumption. Faith is preparing the soil, planting the seed, weeding, watering, protecting. These actions follow the principles laid out for us in the Bible. Having done the work God has instructed and empowered us to do, we may exercise faith by believing that God will bring forth the fruit. Examples of presumption include throwing the seeds on a bare patch of ground and expecting God to do the rest, or conversely, thinking that we are the ones who can actually make the fruit grow.

Pam and I were confident of God's calling to leave the security of the salaried job. This confidence came through much study of God's inspired word, and many hours on our knees in prayer. We were tempted to be afraid, but, we were willing to do whatever He called us to do—as long as we knew it was His will.

Many people plan and order their own lives without ever stopping to ask, "Lord, what would You have me to do?" (Acts 9:6). That, in my mind, is the most dangerous kind of presumption.

⁓⁓⁓⁓⁓⁓⁓⁓⁓⁓⁓⁓⁓

The decision was final! Reluctantly, the board accepted John's resignation. It was a bittersweet time for us: We were excited about following the Lord's plan for our family. At the same time it was painful to our compliant natures to disappoint those we loved and respected. I realize they were only thinking of our good. It is easy to understand that John's resignation did not look like a wise decision. He quit a good job when he had a family to provide for. We had no good answer for them when they asked what we expected to do next.

We appreciated the love and concern. At the same time, we *knew* we were following God's leading, and this gave us the ability to press on. We found comfort in biblical examples of men who chose to do "foolish" things in obedience to God's call. Like Abraham, we knew that God was calling us. Like Abraham, we did not know where the call would lead. Our hearts longed for more direction and clarity, but in God's all-knowing wisdom, He asked us to trust Him without knowing the next step.

"COME BE A FOOL AS WELL"

In a song entitled "God's Own Fool," Michael Card sings, "It seems I've imagined Him [Jesus] all of my life as the wisest of all of mankind, but if God's holy wisdom is foolish to man, He must of seemed out of His mind."

When you follow God, it is almost guaranteed to look foolish (at best) to the world looking on. Think of Noah building the ark, Abraham moving to "who knows where," Joshua marching around Jericho, David attacking Goliath, and the list goes on. When we read the Bible we already know "the rest of the story" behind these great Biblical narratives. They don't look so foolish from our vantage point. But, if you were Noah's contemporary, how would you counsel Him about pouring his whole life savings into the ark?

There's a lot of theoretical talk today about faith. The men of old learned to walk by faith in a very practical way, and God requires no less from us. Is my faith in God, or is it in my job, my bank account, or my insurance policies? Would I walk away from it all if I knew God was calling me to do so?

We felt that calling, and praise God, **He** gave us the faith to go forward. Although it was the most difficult and challenging thing we have ever done, it was also the most precious and rewarding. God became our comforter and counselor; prayer became the breath of our souls; food and clothing became gifts from God. We wouldn't trade the experience for all of Donald Trump's wealth!

Card's song goes on to challenge each of us, "So we follow God's own Fool, for only the foolish can tell. Believe the unbelievable, come be a fool as well."

Do this and you'll be in great company with all of the other "fools" found in Hebrews 11!

In April, we moved into our cute little log cabin by the creeks. It was not finished but it was close enough, and we were eager to get settled. Several members of our kind and loving church family came that day to give us a hand. We started to settle into our new physical surroundings, but our minds were still unsettled. "What's next, Lord?"

Reflecting on the years since leaving Africa, we felt a little confused. Why did we take the time and money for John to get his master's degree if he was going to leave teaching? Why did we build on the farm where we could not easily sell our house? The passage of time usually gives answers to such questions, but in the moment God often allows us to wait in faith. Trusting God is a choice. We chose to trust.

CHAPTER 4

The "Wilderness" Story Begins

SUMMER 1997–SUMMER 1998

February 29, 1996

[Five days after Joshua's birth and 11 months before John resigned]

Heavenly Father, we lay our future before You. We feel the need of a "wilderness" experience. If this is really our need, then lead us to it!

How? What? When? and Where? These were the pressing questions on our minds in June of 1997. We received our last paycheck but still had no direction about what to do next. Searching for answers, we pursued any and every possibility. We knew that God would show us, but we had our own time-table. We expected Him to tell us right away. Oh, how difficult it is for human beings to rest and wait on the Lord! But the waiting time is when we learn the real meaning of surrender. We longed to know the Lord's will. The only way we could learn His way was to spend much time alone with Him. Some of the early impressions from the Lord were hard for me to accept, but my heart was in the right place and I truly wanted to surrender all.

Seek Ye First the Kingdom

In the spring of 1997, as we braced to receive our last paycheck, I was spending much time wrestling with God . . . "What am I going to do?" "How am I going to provide for my family?" "How do the bills get paid?"

Then, in the clearest communication that I have ever "heard" God speak, the impression came to my heart, "You are not to focus on earning a living. You are to focus on serving." Of course! The answer was so obvious in hindsight. This was one of the great lessons in Christ's Sermon on the Mount (Matthew 5–7). Don't worry about what you're going to eat or drink or wear. Your Heavenly Father knows what you need. But "seek ye first the Kingdom of God and His righteousness [service], and all these things shall be added unto you" (Matthew 6:33).

My burden was lightened and my focus was changed. I wish I could say that my focus has never blurred, but I can say that life is more enjoyable and exciting when you're serving!

"Service! How is that going to pay the bills?" my fearful self kept wondering. The financial stress was on. I felt that the answer was for John to have gainful employment—from home, of course. The Lord dealt with me on this issue. He showed me very clearly that John's impressions were correct. We were not to focus on monetary gain, but on service instead. Our efforts to leave the "gainful employment" expectations in God's hands have been imperfect, but the Lord has routinely brought these ideas back to our attention. Again and again God has placed us in situations where we must choose between service and monetary gain. What He wants is our service. He has no shortage of finances.

The summer of 1997 we did some contract work for my father who was installing conveyor systems. He had several jobs out of state and they paid very well. This brought in the needed funds to make it through those first few months. Campgrounds near the job sites enabled us to be together as a family. Those "camping" weeks were fun. The jobs provided for the basics and we continued to watch and pray for God's guidance regarding our future.

After the teaching job ended, we heard one question over and over. "What are you going to do now?" We could give only one answer. "We are in God's waiting room."

What else could we say? God called. We answered. Now He was silent. God's silence tests our true level of surrender. When we don't get a quick answer, we naturally barge ahead with what we think is best. But we didn't want to do that anymore. Although the waiting time was difficult, we chose to embrace it and be at peace. We longed to be spirit-led, God-directed. We did not want to be job and circumstance driven. We were new to this unsettled state, but we were serious about waiting on the Lord this time. We must not give Him human deadlines.

WAITING ON GOD

We hate to wait! In a society of fast food, fast transportation, and fast Internet we expect fast answers. I encourage you to do a Bible study on the word "wait," because God says we need to do it.

Why wait? I can think of at least a couple of good reasons:

1. Waiting builds faith. One of God's greatest desires is for us to trust Him 100 percent. When we don't get quick answers, it exercises and strengthens our "faith muscle."

2. Waiting reveals who is really on the throne of our heart. There is a classic illustration of this in 1 Samuel 13. King Saul was to wait for Samuel to come and offer sacrifices. Samuel was later than Saul wanted him to be, so the king went ahead and did it himself. In doing so, he lost the kingdom. All because he wouldn't wait on God's timing.

Like Saul, we often wait impatiently for a time, but before long we mutter, "I *can't* wait any longer. I'm just going to have to do what I think is best." Then we blindly plunge forward. We need to ask ourselves a very serious question. Is our impatience worth so much that we are willing to lose the kingdom over it?

Our testimony is that God *will* answer. But He will answer in *His* time. In the meantime . . . "wait on the Lord!"

Late that summer we had a pleasant surprise. My older brother's family found a lovely country property forty-five minutes from our home and moved into our area. Because it was an old house, they wanted to do some remodeling. They asked John if he would be willing to work for them. Though this situation did not fit into our long-term goal of having John at home, it did provide a means of income during our time of waiting. For the first year, that job provided for us. Unlike the teaching job, it allowed John to leave work and come home each day when the five o'clock quitting time came. The Lord was slowly weaning us from dependence on external sources of support.

Whenever we start doing what God wants us to do, the enemy starts to send out decoys. Our first tempting "decoy" offer appealed to one of our treasured long-term interests. We've always been interested in working with families. We were passionate about raising our own family, and we believed that the Lord wanted us to help and encourage other families when the time was right. But the time was not yet right.

We received an offer of a generous monthly stipend if we would focus on family ministry. The stipend was sufficient to supply our basic needs, so our first thought was, *God's leading is amazing!* We were thrilled with the thought of being paid to do something we were so passionate about. We could spend our days raising our own children while preparing materials that would encourage and support the "Jerusalem First" idea!

But God had other plans. I praise God He was able to cut through our excitement, get our attention, and give us the clear word that this was not His timing. Prayerfully we waited and continued to look at the few options that came to us. I was surprised to find the following entry in my journal as it differs from what I "remember."

November 16, 1997

Good evening, Lord. I'm alone! Amazing peace and quietness. John is gone, the children are all snug in their beds and here I sit relaxing by the wood stove. Am I too complacent about the lack of money for paying bills? We want to be Spirit-led and not job-driven. John keeps coming back to the idea of gardening and I love that idea. It would be a real service while giving us the opportunity to encourage simple living.

"Experimental religion" is an exciting but difficult school. It is like taking a science lab with no human instructor. The first year after John quit teaching established a repeating pattern of hard times. Money was extremely tight. Our first bills went past due, which we didn't believe would happen. When the Bible says, "My God shall supply all your need" (Philippians 4:19), I truly believed that meant we would always have money to pay our bills by the day they were due. That was not our experience. But our phone and electricity were never turned off. We always had the money in time to avoid being disconnected!

From the very beginning, we chose to believe that we were learners, and that these difficult experiences were God's workmen, training us for heaven (Ellen White, *Acts of the Apostles*, p. 524).

March 18, 1998

Father, I long for Your peace! I choose not to be anxious. Lord, help me to be willing and happy, even when scraping the bottom of the barrel. Even if it's for the rest of my life. You know what we need, and I pray that I can bear my trials cheerfully. Thank You for the opportunity to stretch my faith.

A whole year after our salary ended we still lacked positive direction. I had my hopes set on John supplementing a gardening income with a part time "real job" that paid "real money." I thought I was surrendered to the Lord's will. In reality I kept hanging onto my own ideas. These ideas often contradicted the Lord's leading.

KNOWING GOD'S WILL

"But how can you know God's will?" is a question we are often asked. Well, how do you know anyone's will? You've got to ask them, right?

These are the steps we try to take when we seek God's direction:

1. Neutralize your own will. It's amazing how often we go to God wanting Him to ratify our decisions rather than saying, "not my will but thine be done." Don't go to God with an agenda. Go with an open heart and mind.

2. Go to God's Word. Obviously you will not find a "thus saith the Lord" for every specific problem you face, but you *will* find principles that can be applied in all situations. These may be found through studying sacred history, searching God's law, topical studies, or applying lessons from the great stories of the Bible. The better you know your Bible, the easier this becomes. Then if you still need clarity and direction:

3. Seek Godly counsel. Go to those whose lives reveal the fruit of the spirit (Galatians 5:22, 23). There is wisdom in an abundance of counselors (Proverbs 11:4).

4. Look for providential circumstances. Sometimes God still works through "signs and wonders" to reveal His will.

5. Recognize His impressions on your heart. We have found that following God's will brings peace. When we are out of His will, there is unrest and tension in the soul.

Just be sure you don't make decisions based solely on the last three. They must line up with numbers one and two! And then remember this is not celestial "Hide and Seek." God really *wants* to reveal His will to you.

July 7, 1998

June 29 & 30 John went to spend the day with the Lord. I have been at home praying for him; I should have been praying more for myself. When he came home and shared with me how the Lord had led, I began to despair!

June 29, 1998

Lord, it's good to come away with You! Thank You for refocusing my mind. I feel like You're telling me that AutoCAD is not a good option—because its goal is not serving, but money.

At this time John was investigating anything that could fit the requirement of providing a living while giving him more time with the family. One possibility was doing computer drawings for a friend who is an architect. After taking an AutoCAD (drafting) class, and making a couple of trips to North Carolina, it became clear that this was not God's plan for us. We were to keep looking for His will, trusting the promises in His word for guidance.

Some friends in our church knew of John's interest in photography and asked him to take some family pictures, which he gladly did. Then others heard and started asking for their pictures to be taken. This got us started down another rabbit trail. John had all the equipment needed, it was something he enjoyed, and on some level, the family could be involved. At the least a child could tag along on photo shoots and be his "assistant." John started getting excited about a photography business. Outdoor portraiture would even keep him out of a studio!

Very quickly the Lord made it perfectly clear to both of us that this was not His plan. John continued to look for God's leading.

=================== *June 29 (continued)* ===================

The only door left open is agriculture, so I will continue to pursue this option until You either close that door or open another one. . . . I should sell my camera and equipment since I know I am not going to pursue photography. . . . [I'll] continue to work two days a week on remodeling until I'm shown what else I should do.

∞∞∞∞∞∞∞∞∞∞∞∞∞∞∞∞∞∞ *July 7 (continued)* ∞∞∞∞∞∞∞∞∞∞∞∞∞∞∞∞∞∞

Again the Lord had said NO to my plans. I badly wanted John to get into AutoCAD to supplement our gardening income. Peace left me and Satan had his way for a day. I looked and felt sullen and unhappy. It seemed the Lord was asking more of us than He had asked others.

Although I was excited about doing some farming, I had some very valid fears. The greatest was financial. The small farm movement had not yet come of age, and most people were skeptical. Current wisdom suggested that nobody could make a decent living on a small family farm. There were precious few people to learn from. My other fears were related to my family. I knew I would be torn between the needs of the farm, the needs of the home, and the homeschooling and child training. Outdoor work has always been more pleasing to me than housework. I feared it would be a constant struggle to make myself do the necessary housework if I had pressing outdoor responsibilities. My husband is a lover of order. A neat and tidy home is important to him!

In mercy, God keeps a veil over the future. He simply asks us to surrender one day at a time. Our main desire was to grow closer as a family while learning to live by faith. The Lord knew what that would take. I wanted the experience, but thankfully I did not understand what it was going to cost.

∞∞∞∞∞∞∞∞∞∞∞∞∞∞∞∞∞∞ *July 7 (continued)* ∞∞∞∞∞∞∞∞∞∞∞∞∞∞∞∞∞∞

On Wednesday [June 30] John gave me some time to seek the Lord. . . . I found some real peace and the joy that comes from a full surrender. John had asked for a sign of rain within the next 24 hours to confirm the calling he felt. . . . It rained! On

Sabbath, I shared with John that the Lord had brought me to perfect peace, excitement, and actual happiness about the idea of farming. I was basking in following the Lord. Then John told me that the second sign he had asked of the Lord was my peace and enthusiasm about farming. . . . Our calling is confirmed.

Father, I praise You and thank You for Your leading in our lives. Thank You for peace . . . forgive me for my anxiety and lack of trust. Thank you for the way You're building our faith!

My husband wisely made a commitment to wait on the Lord until we could move forward as a united team. He made sure I had time to seek the Lord about our options. Looking back, I can see that if he had pushed on with the farming plans, thinking *she'll eventually see the light in this*, it could have destroyed the very things we were attempting to gain.

===================== *July 21, 1998* =====================

Dear Lord, it's my 35th birthday today, and it seems like an appropriate time for reflection. What have I accomplished in my life? Am I stronger in my Christian walk? Am I in Your will? We've really gone out on a limb for You, Lord. No home or health insurance. No retirement or savings account. No steady income and no prospects in the future for having one. From the world's point of view, we're crazy! How about from Your point of view? All I want is the assurance of Your presence and blessing. I want to serve You with all my heart, soul, and strength. I want to be a radical witness for You. I want my motto to be "seek ye first the kingdom of God and His righteousness and all these things shall be added unto you."

The only open doors that I see before me are: (1) serving my family—the work that lies nearest—and (2) agriculture. I'm confident of Your will in the first area, but I guess I'm like Gideon in the second area—I keep needing signs. You know it's my heart's desire, but is it Yours? Will it be too all-consuming? Will it be a god to me? Will it leave time for other outreach? . . . Help me not to get so consumed with agriculture that I don't have time or energy for whatever You might call me to do.

Our own personal Red Sea experience was now behind us. The wilderness experience we thought we needed was before us.

CHAPTER 5

"Success"

SUMMER 1998–SPRING 1999

God wanted us to farm. Getting that information was the first step. What, exactly, did that mean? How should we make it happen? We had no resources. We knew nothing about farming. Hard work was not something we were accustomed to. These were the obvious facts. Other realities were not so clear to us yet. God intended to redefine our vocabulary. We must let go of our preconceived notions about the meaning of "needs" and of "success."

A farmer must have a market crop. We seriously explored the idea of growing garlic. Someone in our county was said to be doing "very well" with garlic, so we looked him up. Who knew that farmers tend to paint the rosiest picture possible when talking to potential farmers! They will tell you about the very best year they ever had but fail to mention the crop failures and hard years. A positive attitude is not a bad characteristic. It's good to focus on the positive! Farmers tend to love what they do—which makes it easy for them to remember the good years and forget the bad. What we wanted, however, was a realistic evaluation of our actual potential for success.

While looking seriously at garlic, we also began considering strawberries. That year the children and I had to travel two hours to pick strawberries grown by an elderly farmer. Since we wanted to learn about farming, I spent quite a bit of time talking to the kind gentleman. The Lord used him to encourage us. He even wrote a long letter in which he described his experience and the details of his strawberry farming methods. We saw this helpful advice as added confirmation from the Lord. After digesting the strawberry man's letter, we went off to visit him and his wife. They kindly embraced our family, and shared freely from their wealth of knowledge and experience.

Back at home, John decided to take the strawberry idea to the Lord, his Senior Partner. Retreating to the hills, he asked God for direction on how to proceed. The thought came that he should ask his brothers if they would invest in our first planting of strawberries. He calculated the costs and the potential returns. On paper it looked like a very low-risk investment.

Approaching his brothers, John asked if they would be interested in investing in our first strawberry crop; ignorance and inexperience blinded us to the vast number of things that could go wrong. We assured our family that it would be a worthwhile investment and they generously cast their lot with us. We began our farming ministry.

Dawn to dark, we worked to prepare for that first crop. We leveled a propagation pad. We built a shade structure to protect the young plants. Because of our ignorance, we made everything from scratch. This was before the Internet so it was not easy to find information or helpful products. Instead of buying nursery trays, we constructed our own. These monstrosities were large enough to hold 288 soil blocks. When full, they weighed approximately seventy pounds, making them so awkward and heavy that it was a two-person job to move them!

We had to have an irrigation timer. That meant we needed power in the barn. Getting power out there was no small task. We needed a simple trench for the wires, so we got out the shovels. But our "simple" task got complicated when we hit solid rock! Then there was the irrigation line for the field to dig and install. We designed a misting system. We set up the timer to regulate the propagation process during the first four weeks. We laid out the strawberry field. Then we plowed, disked, harrowed, and hauled rocks out. We hauled a lot of rocks. It was a red-letter day when we ordered our first plants. We also ordered all the materials to make our own potting mix. Yes, we actually mixed forty-five wheelbarrow loads of potting mix to plant eighteen thousand plants. Everyone else used plug trays. We decided to use a soil blocking method to keep the plants from getting root bound. John formed those two-inch blocks a dozen at a time. Because of his inexperience, this took at least forty hours. We pushed eighteen thousand little runners into the blocks, one at a time.

Planting cannot be delayed, but we still had a home and three young children to care for. The young ones were then two, four, and six years of age. Did I mention that John still had a one-hour commute two days a week to finish that remodeling project I mentioned earlier? Oh, and we had six weeks to accomplish everything! It's exhausting to just to think about those days!

The strawberry project marked an important phase in our spiritual and physical education. We started to learn how to lay hold of God's promised strength for the big tasks. "He giveth power to the faint: and to them that have no might He increaseth strength" (Isaiah 40:29). We also learned that God is not short on helpers when He sees fit to send them. The willing help of our friends and family made the difference between success and failure. Many loving hands helped us to accomplish the propagation of all eighteen thousand plants. Those loving hands were there four weeks later when those plants were ready to transplant, one at a time, by hand, into the field. An insurmountable mountain was conquered. John saw many reasons to be confident that the Lord was leading.

God's Leading and Blessings

In the fall of 1998 we decided it was time to give God's farm a name. After much thought and prayer, we decided to call it "Bountiful Blessings Organic Farm." The list below is by no means complete, but it gives some idea of the blessings that led us to choose the name.

1. Unexpected donation of tractor implements.
2. We were led to build down by the creek which was close to the land we would be farming (this was not our hearts' desire as far as location).
3. God uses others, whom we would not have expected, to encourage us in pursuing agriculture.
4. God brought quotes and texts to our attention which pointed out the blessings of agriculture.
5. God "wets the fleece" by sending rain as a sign and also giving Pam peace about focusing on agriculture.
6. Brothers want to invest money in the farm—right when it's needed badly.
7. Friends and family volunteer a Sunday to help—right at a critical time.
8. While I'm sick for a week, my cousin willingly works in my place.
9. We pass trench and electrical inspections in spite of misgivings.
10. Electricity is hooked up and shade cloth is delivered on Friday—a direct answer to prayer.
11. Friends and parents volunteer to help plant.
12. The weather cooperates beautifully.
13. Neighbor offers free hay/straw.
14. Family members offer to help with deer fencing (on the very day we were praying for it).

Yes, God was giving every indication we were to put our hand to the plow. We knew that doing so meant that there must be no looking back except for the purpose of remembering His leading. This decision was put to the test when John's parents asked him to accompany them on a three-week trip to Russia. While praying about this possibility, we were reminded that our first call was to serve. We were very serious about following that call. It was a sacrifice of both time and money, but we felt God was asking us to step out in faith.

At the end of August, between the time of propagating the strawberries and the time for planting them in the field, John made the trip. While in Russia, Mom and Dad inspired medical professionals with ideas on health evangelism and John gave them teaching tools to aid in this work.

It was a long three weeks for the children and me. The pocketbook was empty, so we ate exclusively from the late summer garden which was getting pretty low. We ate potatoes and okra, and then okra and potatoes. After that we ate more of the same, meal after meal. I didn't even like okra, but it was better than nothing at all. We were lonely and the food was monotonous, but God was there to comfort us. Just then He provided us with a wonderful distraction.

Near our house a sweet little gnat catcher built a tiny nest. We discovered her presence one day when we found her three tiny babies on the ground below the nest. They were nothing more than three little puffs the size of cotton balls. Upon further inspection we discovered a poorly constructed little nest with a hole in the bottom. No wonder the babies fell through! We accepted the challenge presented by the helpless little lives in our hands. Our days were already busy, but now we added a strenuous feeding schedule. Three baby birds had to eat every twenty to thirty minutes. For the first few days we kept them in a cage in the house where they reminded us to feed them regularly. Soon we decided that our little friends would benefit from some sunshine and fresh air so we began taking the cage outside and setting it on the porch railing.

One day we heard the babies chirping energetically. To our surprise, another bird flew up and clung to the side of the cage. The newcomer reached through the bars and fed one of the babies. Soon our guest returned and fed another hungry little baby. That faithful mother had not forgotten her young ones! She took back the full responsibility for their care. We started to leave the cage door open so the little mother could fly in and feed her brood. Slowly the children earned her trust. It's hard to believe, but before long the children could hold those baby birds in their hands while the mother came to feed them. It was a little foretaste of Heaven!

There are countless benefits that come to families who raise children in the country, but the one we enjoyed most was the opportunity to be in close contact with God's creation.

John returned just in time to start transplanting those eighteen thousand strawberry plants into the field. It took us a full week to finish the job. When it was done, we mistakenly assumed our work was done until spring. How wrong we were!

From the beginning we read whatever we could find about raising strawberries. We cornered every farmer who might be able to give us more information about our task. Unfortunately, there was not much guidance for the kind of farming we believed in. To our knowledge, nobody in the Southeast had ever tried to grow organic strawberries commercially. Then, to make our job even more difficult, we had chosen to plant without using plastic on the beds. This was good for the environment, but very hard on us!

We chose to use an annual method; planting in the fall, harvesting in the spring, then tilling the plants back into the soil. All of the large farms in this part of the country were moving to this annual method, but they planted on plastic. Organic farming was a totally foreign concept to every farmer we talked to—especially for strawberries! "I don't think you can do that" was the typical response. Disease and weeds are the biggest challenges to strawberry production, and there was literally no one to mentor or teach us how to do this organically.

The weeds started to grow as soon as we set out our plants. We were so naïve that we never questioned the "wisdom" of the person who told us the weeds would all die when they were hit by the first frost. Imagine our dismay when the first frost left our weeds just as green and happy as before the freeze! We consoled ourselves with the thought that it probably wasn't a hard enough frost. But even hard frosts that came night after night failed to discourage those pesky weeds. If anything, they looked even more healthy and vigorous. Our precious little plants were now competing for nutrients with an amazingly healthy crop of weeds.

We made some feeble efforts to conquer the weeds, but they were already so well established that it was difficult work. The children played by our sides as we worked, but that was about as much help as they could contribute. John was working three days a week at my brother's now, so he had very little time to work on the strawberries. Looking back, I realize that there was more we could have done, but we were "green" at this point. I knew little of hard work, perseverance, or diligence. Sitting at the top of those three-hundred-foot rows, hot tears of despair spilled down my cheeks. The weed problem seemed utterly overwhelming.

Weeds were not the only threat to our crop. In November, the deer discovered the tasty green cafeteria we had established (so far as they were concerned) just for them. Of course they were not interested in helping us by eating the lush winter weeds. Oh no! They much preferred a delicious dessert of green strawberry leaves in the dead of winter. Every night we marched around our strawberries, singing, praying, and trying numerous "remedies" to deter the deer. None of our ideas worked for more than a night or two. Deer are very intelligent. They quickly overcame each of our deterrents. Next thing we knew, they were back in the patch, enjoying and destroying our crop.

How we prayed! By the end of January the Lord answered those prayers by providing the money to erect a deer-proof fence (see blessing 14 on page 49). The fence brought an end to the deer's dessert. Sadly, however, the damage was largely done. First the weeds, then the deer. The "one, two" punch knocked us to our knees. Our prospects looked very discouraging.

Early in our strawberry-farming experience, I received an unexpected gift from a high school friend with whom I kept in touch occasionally. The title of the book she sent was, *We Would See Jesus*, published by Christian Literature Crusades. In the providence of God, that little book provided us with spiritual food that nourished us and refocused our faith over and over during that difficult time. To this day, I find strength and courage in the pages of *We Would See Jesus*.

=== *January 9, 1999* ===

It is good to be with You, Lord! I've taken this day off to spend with You, and I've felt You speak to my heart. I've read the book, *We Would See Jesus*. What a blessing! I feel like You've gently shown me that my focus has been wrong. I've been seeking Your will, Your guidance, and Your blessing instead of just seeking You. . . . Today You have shown me that You are everything I need. You don't give it to me, You are it. You are the great I AM (I AM everything you need).

This was the lesson the Lord continued to teach us over and over. Again during that "strawberry spring," He brought the lesson closer to home than ever before. Intellectually, we assented to the fact that God was all we needed, but in reality, we often found ourselves making other things our focus. We mistakenly thought we needed money and, yes we did, but if that is our focus instead of Jesus, we are not seeking the kingdom of God first. We must learn to seek Jesus with our whole hearts. If we do this, "all these things shall be added unto you" (Matthew 6:33). Knowing Him *is* ALL we need. He feeds and clothes the creatures He has put in this world, and He promises to do the same for us. He may see that it is best for us to have the simplest of food and clothing, and this test can reveal what earthly things take His place in our hearts. Every time John and I get focused on other "things," God reminds us that He *is* ALL we need!

NEEDS OR NEED?

In our modern society, the marketing industry has done a fabulous job of convincing us that we need all sorts of things, from a new brand of toothpaste to that shiny SUV.

Those of us who think we are immune to the infectious disease of greed and covetousness might laugh at the ads and feel smug in our "simple" lifestyles. But we still have a fairly substantial list of "basic needs" that must be met each month.

In a text we often misquote, Paul promises, "But my God shall supply all your need [singular, not plural]" (Philippians 4:19).

God is teaching us that we really only have one need—and that is Christ Jesus. When we don't have Jesus, all the world has to offer will never satisfy. When we have Christ on the throne of our hearts we "have it all"!

<hr>

Our crop of winter weeds continued to grow. In the spring it was joined by many varieties of summer weeds. We could see the plants were setting fruit and we just knew that our faith would give us a crop through the weeds. Here we learned a life-long lesson about the relationship between faith and works in the Christian life.

April 28, 1999

Oh, Father! You are the Master Gardener and we need Your wisdom! From man's point of view this strawberry crop is a failure! How can we harvest anything with weeds a foot tall? I choose to believe that You, in Your love, are going to bring something worthwhile out of our weed patch, but what is our part? An acre of weeds is overwhelming with just hand tools! What are we to do?

I was determined to have faith to believe that God would not let us down. To me that meant we would harvest a crop of strawberries. God led us to plant those strawberries, didn't He? We did the best we could, didn't we? Surely God wouldn't embarrass Himself by letting us fail while following His lead! I felt confident that He would miraculously bring a beautiful crop out of our weed patch! That is what I thought success should look like.

May 5, 1999

Dear Father in Heaven, You know my heart . . . John thinks the berry crop is a complete failure. He spent the day with You and the things You told him sent me into a tail spin. Because of the failure of the berry crop, he feels that he should continue the remodeling job three days a week instead of doing a market garden this year. Father, I thought You led us to farm! Why did the strawberries fail? Why does John have to work away from the farm? How will we ever build a viable business here?

I choose to believe that You will still bring a strawberry crop out of those weeds, but John doesn't even want to weed-eat the patch so we can find the berries that I know You want to give us. . . . If we could just have a direct "Thus saith the Lord to John and Pam Dysinger!" Father, I will try to let go of my preconceived ideas and follow the best I know. . . . Give me peace . . . lift me up where I can see more clearly. . . . [I'm] longing to be a faithful servant, a cheerful follower.

My determined "faith" that God would make a profitable crop out of that weed patch did not make it happen. My hopes were dashed! I struggled with the Lord like never before. Hundreds of hours of hard work went into getting that crop in the ground. Many more hours were spent in feeble attempts to reclaim the plants from the weeds. I could not see any good reason why the Lord allowed things to fall apart like this. It was a hard, humbling, embarrassing blow. In time I learned that the great strawberry debacle was a valuable and important lesson that we needed for the future success of our farm and our characters.

The strawberries taught us a vivid lesson about getting weeds out of our gardens and our hearts when they are small. What you get out of the ground correlates directly with the well-directed effort you put into it. Had God honored my prayers and given us that miracle crop, we would not have understood the balance between our part of the work and God's part. Our job is to do all we can to create an environment conducive to growth. Having done our part we trust, because only God can cause the seed to germinate. Farming gives us a perfect picture of the relationship between faith and works. Faith without works is dead—just like our first crop. God could not honor our faith because we did not combine it with corresponding works. We must use the six days God created for work and do what needs to be done, when it needs to be done, no matter what it takes.

This does not mean we have become workaholics! This is about timeliness. The old saying, "A stitch in time saves nine" is good counsel for the farmer as well as for the seamstress. This means putting in long hours at certain times of the year. Doing these difficult tasks as a family is tiring, but it is also gratifying! The bigger the task, the greater the need for creativity, ingenuity, efficiency, and plain hard work. A completed task brings a corresponding sense of satisfaction and sweet rest. Instead of weakening us, the difficult, diligent work makes us stronger.

Looking back, we are thankful that God did not answer my prayers the way I thought He should. If God had made a beautiful strawberry crop out of our weed patch, we would have missed out on some vitally important spiritual lessons. So, was our first strawberry crop a success? We say, "Yes!" God rewrote our definition of success!

CHAPTER 6

Trust, Delight, Commit, and Rest

SUMMER 1999–SPRING 2000

Have you ever been at a loss about how to accomplish something that you just knew you were supposed to do? That's how we felt in the summer of 1999. By faith, we talked about planting our second crop of strawberries, but we had no visible means by which to accomplish the task. We clung to the promises; "Trust in the Lord. . . . Delight thyself also in the Lord. . . . Commit thy way unto the Lord; trust also in Him; and He shall bring it to pass. . . . Rest in the Lord, and wait patiently for Him" (Psalm 37:3–7).

We were committed to take all our needs to the Lord only, and let Him work out the details. It wasn't always easy to keep our needs unknown to those around us. At this point we had seven families of relatives living close by. All of us attended the same church. This was a blessing in many ways, but it did make it difficult to quietly bear some of the things the Lord was taking us through. Sometimes we wished that we could live where no one else could see us struggling. We felt like we needed to protect God's reputation. We didn't want others to be discouraged from following Him based on what we were going through.

Looking back, I realize that pride was our real issue. God was humbling us and teaching us to live to please Him alone. This was very hard on my people-pleasing ego. God knew that the most effective way to deal with our pride was to keep us in close association with those we loved—those from whom we most wanted respect and approval. The lack of funds to plant a second crop of strawberries tested our resolve to leave our reputation and God's fully in His capable hands.

And then the phone rang. "Pam, do you have the money to plant your strawberry crop this fall?"

I stammered around, not sure how to respond. *Just be honest,* was the thought that came to mind. "No, we don't," I admitted with some embarrassment.

"I will send you a check tomorrow!" said the voice on the other end of the line. I was speechless! I prayed and tried to remember if, in any way, I had taken our situation out of God's hands by talking about it to anyone, but I had not. This was just God, Himself, confirming clearly that we were supposed to plant that second crop. I couldn't wait to tell John!

The many lessons from our first year's "weed patch" were fresh in our minds. We were determined not to repeat the same mistakes. The infrastructure was in place, so propagating and planting came much easier this time. My dad started a wonderful tradition. He came in August and September each year to help with the propagating and planting. How encouraging it was to have the extra set of willing hands to help us get the crop into the field. Those were happy days with fond memories! Shared labor creates many opportunities for meaningful communication. We all bonded in special ways as we prepared the strawberry plants for the field.

We put our very best efforts into the strawberries that second year. John had more time to devote to the farm. He still did some fence building and other off-site work for a neighbor, but this produced only a meager amount of money. God was continuing to re-define our definition of the word "need."

September 28, 1999

Father, I need Your peace; peace when the house is a clutter and I'm down on myself. Peace when things get lost, peace when I see my children wearing old, torn clothes, peace when the bills are overdue, peace as the staples in our cupboards vanish. Peace, peace, wonderful peace.... When I think of the problems, I'm very discouraged, but when I'm focused on You there is peace. "Thou wilt keep Pam in perfect peace when her mind is stayed on You; because she trusts in You."

If John works on weeding, how will we pay the bills; but if we are paying the bills, how will we have time to weed? Should I get out and do more weeding? I struggle so much to keep my home duties done and take care of the children.

November 11, 1999

Father, thank You for peace. As the food supply dwindles, You encouraged me with the thought, "It's not all gone." I was thrilled to get some fresh items for the first time in a long time. We have what we need for today and we'll trust You to supply for tomorrow.

Through the fall and winter, we struggled to find the balance between working on the strawberries and trying to pay the bills. We worked long and hard to keep the plants from being overcome by weeds, and we succeeded with two-thirds of our acre. We were still very much at the beginning of the learning curve.

As we faced the year 2000 (Y2K), there was widespread fear and uncertainty. People stockpiled food and supplies just in case we lost all power, and life as we knew it changed drastically. Many of our friends made elaborate and expensive purchases to prepare for whatever calamity might come at midnight on December 31, 1999. That was not the case at our house! There was no money to buy even food for the next week! Candles, matches, batteries, non-electric gadgets, and extra toilet paper did not fill our storage closets. They were empty and we were putting our complete trust in the Lord! People all over our nation anxiously rang in the new year while we slept peacefully in our little log cabin by the creek. On New Year's Eve, we had reflected on stories from Scripture that tell how God provided food for His people through the birds of the air, the multiplication of the loaves and fishes, and the Heavenly manna. Each story gave us hope. God's arm is just as long today as it was in the time of Moses. We rested in the peaceful knowledge that our bread and water would be sure—no matter what happened to the world around us.

We longed to learn how to hear God's voice speaking to our hearts on a more regular basis. The Bible says, "And thine ears shall hear a word behind thee, saying, This is the way, walk ye in it, when ye turn to the right hand, and when ye turn to the left" (Isaiah 30:21). We wanted to become better acquainted with this "still small voice" (1 Kings 19:12). We knew He was speaking to us, but hearing and understanding require much quiet time with Him.

HEARING GOD'S VOICE

"When every other voice is hushed, and in quietness we wait before Him, the silence of the soul makes more distinct the voice of God. He bids us, 'Be still, and know that I am God'" (Ellen White, *The Desire of Ages*, p. 363).

I'm convinced that we fail to hear God's voice clearly because we rarely experience silence in the soul. We seem to be afraid of that silence. In the car, the radio is on; at home, the television is on; when we are walking, the earbuds are on. All the while, the Lord is trying to get our attention, but His voice is drowned out by the white noise of modern life.

Elijah, on Mount Horeb, experienced this problem (1 Kings 19). There was a great wind, but the Lord was not in the wind; after the wind an earthquake, but the Lord was not in the earthquake; after the earthquake a fire, but the Lord was not in the fire. Then, there was a still small voice, and Elijah recognized the voice of God.

Sometimes our lives can feel as topsy-turvy as a whirlwind and as urgent as a fire, but Jesus speaks to us through the storm, "Peace, be still."

No, I've never heard Him speak audibly, but His still small voice speaks to the soul in ways that are distinct and clear. At first, you may not recognize the voice, but as you accustom your soul to silence, the voice becomes louder.

How do you know it's the voice of God and not the voice of the enemy? Two simple tests:

1. It must agree with the laws and principles of the Bible. God does not contradict Himself.

2. If it crosses your will and causes death to "self," then it's very likely God's voice. If it feeds your "flesh" and carnal nature, then it's not from Him.

Shhhhh, listen! . . . Do you hear Him speaking? He's whispering to you, "Be still, and know that I am God."

January 19, 2000

[While visiting and working for Pam's parents in NJ]

Dear Lord, I just want to pause to thank You for Your leading in the "little things" in life. . . . Last night, out of the blue, You impressed me long after I had gone to bed that I had not hooked up Mom & Dad Ivins disposal correctly. I got up and fixed the problem just before the dishwasher would have overflowed! Thank You, Lord!

I also think of the time I went to Midas to pick up our locked car—without taking the spare key. You gave me peace about it, and when we arrived, the back door was unlocked!

Then there was the time we had borrowed the Crews' pickup truck to go to Lowe's. Jonathan accidentally locked the truck with the keys inside and the engine running! The checkout man came up and tried an old Ford key he had in his wallet—and the door opened! He said the key was from a Ford Mustang he'd had years before—and he had just never taken it out of his wallet! Thank You, Lord! These are just a few of the lessons we are learning on listening and trusting. You do answer prayer!

Dear Lord, I come to you this morning again questioning what You would have us to do. The farming just seems like a hole we're digging for ourselves. I don't want to go into debt, but I'm not sure what else to do.

Lord, I've read this morning that I have "partnership" with You (1 John 1:3, George Müller's interpretation). May I trust in You more fully and completely. Give me faith, I pray.

By March the strawberry plants were looking beautiful, though we never did get that last one-third acre weeded. We were hopeful the Lord was going to give us a bountiful crop. But we were about to face one of the biggest enemies of strawberries: FROST! Strawberries flower very early, so they fall easy prey to damaging spring frosts. This time we were prepared, or so we thought!

Ideally, strawberries are frost protected with an overhead sprinkler system. But overhead sprinkler systems are very expensive. We opted for the more affordable protection of floating row covers. This means covering the whole field with a fabric that is similar to dryer sheet material. It gives three or four degrees of protection.

The afternoon of April fifth, the whole family got out in the field and pulled the floating row covers over the crop. After doing all we could do to protect the crop, we gathered together, wrapped our arms around each other, and asked God to protect our berries. Confidently we walked home, feeling secure in the fact that we had done our part and trusting God to do His part.

Our first thought the next morning was, *What is the temperature?* Opening the front door, John was blasted with cold air. His heart sank as his eyes rested on the face of the thermometer, 22 degrees! All we could do was drop to our knees, asking the Lord to give us peace no matter what the outcome. After the sun burned the frost off and the covers dried, we anxiously walked out to the field to confirm what we *knew:* the Lord had protected our crop and there would be no damage. Doesn't *talking* faith count as faith?

Pulling back the covers, we were faced with the gut-wrenching reality that our crop had NOT been spared. Everywhere we looked our beautiful little yellow flowers had turned the black color of death. We could hardly believe our eyes! How could the Lord allow this to happen? Our overwhelmed humanity brought up a multitude of questions and very few answers. Crushed, we staggered home to wrestle with God. Had eight months of hard work, along with all of our hopes and dreams died in one night?

Back on our knees we struggled to reach that quiet place where we could wait in silence before the Lord. Slowly, God began to speak to our hearts in a voice we could recognize. "Do you *really* need those strawberries, or do you need Me? I want to be your ALL."

"You're right, Lord," we acknowledged, "You are all we need!"

Surrender was sweet. Peace returned. God had called us to this and He had promised that our bread and water would be sure. Would we choose to be content with bread and water?

Two days later, we again pulled the covers over the berries. The Lord had restored our peace and we felt confident He would bless our efforts. We again prayed that whatever was left of the crop would be protected. More than this, we prayed that we would have peace no matter what. We asked only that the Lord would be glorified.

John and I rose early to pray as usual. We were both praying when we looked to see the temperature. The thermometer read 25 degrees. We knew all too well that the row cover was not enough protection without divine aid. By nine o'clock in morning the sun had burned off the moisture and the covers were dry. I anticipated a miracle, but John was not ready to face his fears.

I prefer to tackle things head-on. I wanted to know the truth, or so I thought. Marching out to the field alone, I started yanking those row covers off. What met my eyes took me to my knees. I deeply regretted having come out alone. Tears streamed down my face. John saw me stumbling back towards the house and knew it was bad news. With outstretched arms, he came out to meet me. Wordless, we just clung to one another, blending our tears and pain, afraid to speak for fear of denying our Lord.

Together we went back out to the field to finish uncovering the berries. It wasn't easy for such novices to estimate crop losses, but we calculated that those two nights of frost killed roughly 50 percent of our crop. We were sorely tempted with feelings of discouragement and abandonment, but the Lord gave us the ability to accept the things we couldn't change. We knew that our Partner had not left us. By faith we trusted He would supply our need. We pressed on, choosing to believe the Lord would bless the remainder of our crop. He was teaching us to trust, rest, and bounce back from our own version of reality—choosing to see that His reality is far different from ours.

Near the end of April, the remaining berries were blushing red. Even though we had suffered major losses, we were encouraged with the fact that there were still many berries to sell, if only we could make it through the often-violent spring weather. John faithfully did his part to protect the crop from damage, but some things are out of a growers' control. Hail is one of those things!

It was late one day when John gathered the family for worship. He told us we were heading for some bad weather with the possibility of damaging hail. Kneeling together, we lifted our petitions to our Heavenly Father, who is always touched by the prayers of His children. Having laid it all before the Lord, we arose with peace in our hearts.

I was upstairs helping the children get ready for bed when John called out to us. "Look out the east window!" he cried. The children beat me to the window. They began oohing and aahing. The golden light of sunset shone below the dark clouds, and the sight that met my gaze brought tears to my eyes. There in the sky was the most beautiful rainbow I have ever seen! It seemed to rest on the hill of our neighbor's property and perfectly arched over our strawberry field before melting into our own hillside. To compound the impact, it wasn't just one rainbow, but a complete double rainbow! In our hearts we felt that the Lord was putting His blessing over the strawberry crop, and also over our whole farm, our whole life, and our whole future. This is the reason that our farm logo had to have God's bow of promise arching over the words, "Bountiful Blessings Farm."

It was spring. The surviving strawberries were ripening. We didn't know how to advertise—how to get the word out that we had strawberries for sale. We contacted two local newspapers to see if they would be interested in stories. To our surprise, they both ran cover articles that proved to be a tremendous blessing. The word was out. A local farm had organic strawberries! The following article appeared on May 8, 2000 in the Hickman County Times:

A Strawberry Livelihood
By Bradley A. Martin

Few folks are jumping full-time into farming these days, though John Dysinger thinks he's found a way to succeed.

"I'm convinced, if you stay small and go organic, you can do it," he says. "We won't get rich, but that's not our goal. Our goal is to sustain our lifestyle."

Towards that end, May is a big month for the Dysinger family: The strawberry crop is coming in, and their one-acre plot at their Leatherwood Community farm is increasingly covered by the sweet, heart-shaped spring fruit.

Since September, 18,000 plants have received daily care from John, his wife Pam and their children Kirsten, 8, Jonathan, 6 and Joshua, 4. Late frost killed some of the berries in early April, but what remains is still a sight to see and sample:

Twenty 300-foot-long rows of flowering green plants, each of which hide the ripening fruit under their skirts. All of it is grown organically – no chemicals, fungicides, pesticides – and almost all of it has been weeded by hand, almost every day.

Strawberries, you see, just don't pop up out of the ground when warm weather arrives. And if it is to be your major source of income – as it will be this season at the Dysingers' Bountiful Blessings Organic Farm – then you work hard around the calendar.

"When it comes down to it," John Dysinger says, "it's a lot of hard weeding. That's why everyone's not doing it, I guess."

The Dysinger's believe they are the only organic strawberry farmers in Tennessee, and quite possibly several other states – maybe all the way to California. How well they will do, and whether the sweet fruit can be a profitable cash crop remains undetermined as the fruit begins to be harvested.

But there is plenty of hope, and faith.

"The Lord is our expert, actually," John says. "We're in partnership with Him, and we have to turn to Him quite often."

John and Pam both served as missionaries and educators in Kenya until coming to Hickman County in 1995. They settled on a piece of his parents' land there, and John became the teacher at Martin Memorial Seventh-day Adventist Church School in Centerville, a satisfying experience, except for one significant dilemma.

"It was too all-consuming," he says, "I wasn't having any time with my family, and I felt convicted that my family was my first priority."

So he resigned and went home. Of course, needs that demand money remained, and Dysinger took the odd, short-term jobs necessary to make those ends meet. And he looked for a way to fulfill his family's needs from close by their log home. Farming was an obvious choice.

"We looked at a lot of different possibilities, but I kept coming back to this," he says. "Agriculture was part of God's original plan ... I figured if you follow God's original plan, you can't get too far off."

For a young family already on a vegetarian diet, strawberries seemed a possible way to go, few folks were doing it; most folks enjoy eating them; children could participate in the work, part of their home-schooling ... and there'd be a built-in reward at harvest time.

"This is our dessert, out in the field," John says. "It's wonderful to be able to have your children work with you, and be home for lunch, and be there if your wife needs you."

Organic farming promotes health, naturally. John will tell you of studies that indicate that of all fruits and vegetables, strawberries contain the highest level of pesticides. That's due to chemicals, including herbicides and fungicides – many of which the Environmental Protection Agency considers as potential sources of cancer.

At Bountiful Blessings, natural corn gluten is a fall fertilizer. After that, it's sun and rain, frost protection as necessary, and the never-ending weed war. This year's strawberry crop actually covers two-thirds of an acre, John says; the weeding is so demanding that the rest of the rows are packed with weeds they couldn't keep clipped, though some berries will emerge from them, too.

Of course, there's always next year. "We hope to have another chance," John says.

Actually, there's still this year: A quarter-acre has been set aside for organically-grown vegetables that will be available for sale; lettuce is ready now. Blueberry and raspberry bushes are being tended, and a set of beehives is next to the strawberry patch, so organic honey may not be far off. A greenhouse is in the planning stages, And

Kirsten's Krunchy Granola is the 8 year old's contribution to the family enterprise.

If growing naturally healthy fruit sounds easy, the Dysingers can tell you a few things. Their first crop, in 1999, turned out to be two 100-foot rows of berries, enough for the family and friends, though not enough to make a living. And there are precious few organic strawberry farms available to provide guidance; statewide there are only 13 strawberry farms, and Bountiful Blessings appears to be the only organic grower.

"We've learned that there are winter weeds and summer weeds," John says, as well as the fact that human effort, not frost, is an effective weed killer – and that deer do truly love strawberry plants.

"We lost most of it due to inexperience," he said of that initial crop. "They say it takes three years to get into something like this."

Well, year two seems to be one of tremendous improvement. An eight-foot fence keeps out the deer. Weeding commenced not long after the strawberry "tips" propagated last summer, were planted in September.

The first fruit was plucked on April 21, and the harvest should last through the month. The Dysingers are eager to have folks come and pick their own berries – by appointment, please – and have touched enough bases to know that there are markets in Nashville that will take what local folks don't buy.

There's also the possibility that the family may erect a roadside stand on Highway 50.

"We'll see this year if there's more demand than supply," John says.

Interesting position the Dysingers are in as spring weather warms. They're on the edge of self-sufficiency, with a sweet crop in the field and more possibilities in the offing. All of that a result of following God and their consciences.

"No question it was a step of faith," says John, about his decision to teach only at home. "We honestly did not know what we would do. But we felt confident that I needed to be the husband, father and priest of the home. We acted on that principle and trusted the Lord."

We were thankful the reporter kept the spiritual focus of the interview. We wanted God to get all the glory!

When the season was over we felt like we had observed a miracle of multiplication. In spite of the losses to frost, the plants produced prolifically! The profits we made on that two-thirds of an acre were a tremendous blessing and encouragement. More than that, it was a blessing to serve our community. We got to know our neighbors. We took an interest in our customers and shared God's unfailing goodness. These opportunities brought joy to our hearts. Some of the first customers were an elderly couple. They came to the house and wanted to pick "a couple quarts." I gave them two carriers that held four quarts each. They insisted they only wanted a couple, but I encouraged them to take them—just in case. They arrived back in about thirty minutes with those baskets overflowing. They had picked about sixteen quarts of strawberries! They exclaimed that these were the most beautiful berries they'd ever seen and so plentiful they just couldn't stop! Repeatedly we heard, "These are the best berries I've ever tasted," or "I haven't had berries like this since I was a child!" We gave the glory to God and also suggested that the organic methods might contribute to their sweetness. "Organic" was a new word to most of our customers back then.

Our journals are totally silent for more than a month during strawberry season. Clearly, we were extremely busy! The plants produced so well that our courage was raised to try again. Of course next year we planned to have a full acre with *no weeds!*

Our goals as a family included learning to trust, delight, commit, and rest in our Heavenly Father's care. Seeking first His kingdom, we found His peace and joy amid the financial pressures. Our hopes were already set on next year's crop, which we *knew* would be even better!

CHAPTER 7

Perspectives

SUMMER 2000–SPRING 2001

Do you think the burdens you bear are heavy? You can be sure that there is someone else in your sphere of influence who is going through even greater difficulties. It was at one of our low points that dear friends of ours experienced a heartache which caused us to see our farming trials as almost minuscule.

Our second crop had been a financial success. It was not all that we had hoped it might be, but at least it gave us the courage and ability to press on. The berry patch brought many new friends into our lives, and more relationships were built when we took produce to a small farmers' market during the summer.

In those days "local" and "organic" produce was not yet popular, so we often sold our produce for conventional prices. Our customer base began to grow. People who saw and tasted the organic difference became convinced of the benefits. These folks were willing to pay a higher price.

Growing and marketing organic produce seemed like a full-time job for our family. But we had to develop the infrastructure as we went, and that was a full-time job too. During the summer of 2001 we began construction on a 30' by 60' greenhouse. We thought this was critical for propagating the strawberry plants, but the Lord had other plans for it in the future. Of course, we were not just thinking of starting strawberries. We could get earlier tomatoes with a greenhouse, and maybe grow bedding plants as well. We were full of ideas, but lacked money to follow through.

We didn't want John to leave the farm for employment so we brainstormed about various money-making options. This led us to the idea of selectively logging our ten acres of land. The forestry department gave us some guidance so we could get the job done right. With educated eyes, they carefully selected the trees we should cut. What a blessing God gave us in our woods! That capital, carefully used, allowed John to stay focused on the farm.

The middle of August was strawberry propagating time. By then we had a leveled pad for the greenhouse. The steel structure was in place, but the end walls were not finished and the plastic was not on it yet. We applied the shade cloth we already had and the structure was perfectly adequate for the job.

One challenge we faced was the fact that it took the better part of a week to plant our eighteen thousand strawberry tips, and they needed to be refrigerated until planting. The first two years we rented space in a convenience store cooler, but this was awkward and inconvenient. We investigated several options and came up with nothing. We didn't have the money to buy anything, so we took it to the Lord and He took it to others. Without our knowledge, my dear sister-in-law, Beccy, raised money from church family and relatives to buy a used walk-in cooler! Their love and care touched our hearts!

I scoured the local papers and found an old cooler an hour and a half away. John was terribly busy so I drove the hour and a half to look at it. Yes, it was old, but it didn't look too bad to me. It seemed to run fine. I bought it.

When the cooler was delivered, my poor husband, who likes everything to be neat and clean, was mortified. In the light of day that cooler looked like an unsightly beast. It sat on two large, dilapidated wooden skids. The green paint was chipped and peeling. To top it all off, the only place we could put the ugly monstrosity was right in plain sight for anyone who drove up to the barn. John was visibly disappointed over my choice, and I was mortified that I had done such a poor job of looking the thing over. To make matters worse, it didn't work right. In despair I called a refrigeration man to come out and take a look at it. He wiggled a few wires and made some minor adjustments. The cooler turned on and ran perfectly for us from then on. Mercifully, that dear repairman did not charge us a penny for his visit, not even for his gas to get out to our farm which is thirty minutes from anywhere. This was another precious token of God's love for us manifested through others. The fact that there was not much we could do about the way the cooler looked aided us both in the humbling process!

Thankful for the ability to refrigerate the strawberry tips, we worked long hours trying to get everything ready to propagate the plants. We were still very new to the growing process and failed to realize how much we were affecting next year's crop by planting so late. The target date for field planting in those days was September 20. The tips need four to five weeks of rooting and growth before they are planted in the field. Our little family worked doggedly at planting all of the little runners. Still, it was the end of August before we completed the task. Friends and family often stopped in to lend a much-appreciated hand, but, we never had enough assistance to take away the lessons we were learning about diligence, teamwork, and persevering through tough jobs.

September 20 came and went without a single plant leaving the greenhouse. They just weren't ready. Long ago we made a pact with the Lord that we would not ask anyone but Him for help. He saw fit not to send help during this time. We were grateful for the purchase of an old tobacco planter. We hoped that this machine would decrease our planting time considerably.

September 28, 2000

Father, we really need some help picking dead leaves off our plants, and getting them into the field. We will ask You and only You to supply our need. You know what is for our best good.

We continued to lay our need for help before the Lord. He seemed to say, *"You need to face this alone."* No help presented itself so we chose to believe the Lord had lessons to teach us about how to conquer monumental tasks. We realized that this experience would refine and define our characters. Confident in the Lord's leading, we determined to tackle the challenges head on. We did not waste time looking for an escape route.

With every passing day, our spring crop was being more and more compromised. The little plants were just not ready, and the window of time for planting them kept shrinking.

It was the first part of October before we finally started planting in the field. Exhaustion clouded our minds and the temptation to discouragement was very real. The morning of October 8, we were, as usual, out early. We were still preparing to plant when a van drove into our driveway. Looking up, I couldn't believe my eyes. My brother Greg rolled down the window and said, "You need some help?"

Tears welled up in my eyes, and cascaded down my cheeks. "How did you know we needed help? I thought you were in Florida!" Greg's business trip was unexpectedly shortened, so he and his family were home early. What a relief! His work force was not huge, but it was just the support and encouragement we needed. The Lord sent a message of love and courage through my brother, and our hearts overflowed with gratitude.

October 10, 2000: A Day to Remember

Getting ready to leave for family camp meeting tomorrow. The only complication: 4,000 strawberry plants still to plant in the field. It all seems impossible.

The planter was off the tractor, and all the adjustments were messed up. The tractor had a flat tire. Then there was a problem in the tractor's steering column. We were finally ready to do some planting around 11:30. We planted our first row then the water valve was broken. John fixed it and the next two rows went pretty well. Greg showed up to help us. John drove the tractor, Kirsten and Jonathan planted, then Greg and I came behind to make sure the strawberries were planted correctly. At 2:00 p.m. we had only three rows in. Then the transplanter broke. Kirsten sobbed out our collective heart-cry: "Now there's no way we can go to camp meeting!" But we prayed, God gave peace, and we pulled together. We planted almost four rows in the next 1½ hours. When I was in fixing lunch, Greg and John came up with a better planting plan. After a hurried lunch John dug the holes, Greg drove the tractor, and one child filled the holes with water. The other two children set out the plants and I planted them. When we damaged the water line and had to make an alternate watering plan, we all managed to laugh about it. By 7:00, as the sun was setting, we put the last plant in the ground.

What a feeling of victory! We stayed on task, we stayed close to Jesus, and we experienced His peace. Our children, though only four, seven, and eight years of age, were a great help. They didn't complain about working hard all day. In fact, they felt very important and valuable because they knew the job could not have been done without them. Those tough times drew us close like nothing else could. The hard jobs taught all of us creativity, ingenuity, and efficiency.

MANUAL LABOR

An unfortunate by-product of the industrial revolution is the attitude that manual labor is degrading. As machines began to replace muscles, "mindpower" became viewed as superior to "manpower." White collar jobs were coveted because they brought higher status, more money, and less dirt under the fingernails.

We are firm believers that true education is "the harmonious development of the physical, the mental, and the spiritual powers" (Ellen White, *Education,* p. 13). "Harmonious" is synonymous with "proportionate" and "symmetrical." Thus it is clear that the best education will *balance* the physical, the mental, and the spiritual powers. Where is that balance today?

Agriculture, shop, home economics, and many physical education programs have been dropped from the curriculum in most schools. More and more emphasis is placed on academics while spiritual life is relegated to a Bible class or two if you're fortunate enough to attend a private Christian school. In the process we have produced a crop of educated fools. Yes, they may be able to pass the placement tests for "professional careers," but can they change a clutch, build a house, or plant a garden? Common sense has become very uncommon, and we are all the losers for it.

What is the solution? A renewed emphasis on physical and spiritual training (radical, isn't it?). I believe that a spiritual education is most effectively learned in the family circle, and in personal time with God. I taught high school Bible classes for six years and am not convinced that spirituality can be taught in the classroom. Having said that, I recognize that it *can* be caught from dedicated teachers! A renewed emphasis on the dignity of manual labor is urgently needed. It is not demeaning to work with your hands! On the contrary, it builds tremendous confidence and self-worth.

I believe that working with your hands (manual labor) is actually the "missing link" in our educational system. The "mental rest" that comes with physical exertion will make students more effective when they do take up the books. It also gives opportunity for quiet—where God can more clearly speak to the soul. From my personal experience and observation, I can testify that a renewed emphasis on physical labor empowers women, and makes men feel more "manly." It's past time to restore the balance!

~~~~~~

God was leading, and we did everything in our power to follow. Meanwhile, He began to plant ideas in our minds regarding future plans for the farm. At this point we were not sure whether these thoughts were God's or our own, so we waited and prayed.

========================= *November 28, 2000* =========================

Dear Lord, this morning the thought came to me that it would be so nice if that young family we met recently, who are interested in farming, and/or Edwin and Jennifer would move nearby so that we could have an organic co-operative. Lord, I don't know if this was from You or not. I just want to pray about it and if it was from You, may You also impress others with this idea. Inshallah! [If the Lord wills!]

Only time would tell, so we tucked this thought into the back of our minds.

Finances were still tight but we learned to be at peace, trusting that God would work things out for us. As children, my brothers and I listened with rapt attention to stories of faith from our grandmother's childhood. My great-grandparents lived on a farm and my great-grandfather was an alcoholic. It was in answer to Great Grandmother's simple faith and trust that God supplied food for the family's empty table, shoes for their bare feet, and miraculous answers to their prayers. We asked our grandma to tell those stories over and over. We never tired of hearing how God answered prayer. The memory of those stories gave me courage and faith to press on when times seemed impossible for us. In the face of privation God had provided for my great-grandmother. I knew He would do the same for me. Our part was to trust and wait with willing hearts to follow God's leading.

========================= *January 29, 2001* =========================

Dear Lord, we need a miracle. We don't have enough money coming in to pay our debts. Father, if something doesn't change, we are going to have to give up the farm. But, I feel that it's really Your reputation at stake here. We got into this because we were trying to follow You. People know about our partnership with You, so our failure will be viewed as Your failure. Lord, I don't care about my reputation, but I am jealous of Yours.

We need some money right away! The phone bill is two months behind! Give me wisdom to know my part. I read this morning in Genesis 18:14, "Is anything too hard for the Lord?" I know it's not, so I claim Your promises today.

Dear Lord, I just want to praise and thank you for your answer to my prayer yesterday. I received a $165 check from Drury's Camera Shop for some of my camera equipment. I had forgotten all about it, but You sent it when I needed it most.

Lord, help me to keep my eyes fixed on You—in spite of the storm raging around us. Give me faith to believe that You will see us through.

In January 2001 we decided our family needed some significant "time out." No, we were not going to sit on the stool in the laundry room, but we were going to simplify our schedule. Finances were extremely tight, life was intense, and we felt the need to focus more intentionally on building a tight family unit. After praying about this, we made some changes.

For three months we chose to have church with the children at home. We do not believe this is God's plan long-term, but for a short time it was a blessing to our family. In addition to this, we stopped attending unnecessary gatherings. We needed to simplify life and pre-pare for our spring farm ministry. Our choices were misunderstood, as we knew they would be, but we felt confident that we were following the Lord's guidance in taking this time apart.

～～～～ GOOD, BETTER, BEST ～～～～

"Good, better, best. Never let it rest until your good is better and your better best." Almost everyone has heard the quote, but have we applied it to our practical Christian walk?

When Pam and I determined to follow God no matter what the cost, we had to cut out lots of good things in our lives to make room for better. Books and music CDs were sorted. We cleaned out our closets, de-cluttered the cupboards, cleared our schedules.

Once we eliminated the "good" to make room for the "better," we took up the greater challenge of getting rid of the "better" in favor of the "best." We're still working on that! Life has a way of filling every crack with activities and things—even good things. But are we reserving time and energy for the best things? It is a constant fight to de-clutter our homes, our schedules, and our minds.

Jesus spoke to this in Luke 10:41, 42. Martha was consumed with the good (maybe even the better), but He declared that Mary had chosen the best. What is He saying to you?

After making this decision, we were challenged by various requests for our time. Then the question was, do we consider these requests individually, or simply say "No" to all of them? We chose to evaluate and pray over each invitation that came up. Most were relatively easy to turn down, but the Lord did not lead us to say, "No" to everything!

Our dear friends, Tom and Nancy Hunt (co-workers and friends from Kenya years), were working at a boarding academy two and a half hours away. Since we were on an extremely tight budget, we did not get together with them very often. Just after our resolve to have three quiet months, Tom called John and asked him to have some weekend meetings at their school in late February. Our first thought was to say "No" and schedule a different time. But we took the request to the Lord. We did not have the money to make the trip, but God reminded us of our call to serve. We were to trust Him for the means to accomplish His assignments. In addition to these thoughts, the Lord impressed us that it would be a blessing for our children to spend time with Tom and Nancy's children. Like Kirsten and Jonathan, Heidi and Donald were born in Kenya. After returning to the States, we added Joshua and they had Benjamin. After praying about it, we accepted the call. We planned to leave home a day early for some special fun, including a "big" bike ride. When we left for the trip, we did not have enough money to get back home but we trusted that God would provide for that which He had assigned.

What a wonderful time we had! Kirsten and Heidi have always been like sisters. Even now they can go for months without talking and then pick right up where they left off. As our older boys spent time together it became clear that they were "two peas in a pod." Donald's outgoing personality, Jonathan's deep and sensitive spirit, along with their common interests, bound their hearts in an enduring friendship. Though they were only seven and nine, they were kindred spirits! Every time we got together, the bonds deepened. We looked forward to seeing our children develop life-long connections with these friends who were born on the same continent, in the same hospital, and delivered by the same Polish doctor. Oh how thankful I am we allowed the Lord to change our plans. As we prepared to return home, we committed to spend more time with these dear friends. Miraculously, our tax return was direct deposited into our bank just in time to fill the gas tank!

March 5, 2001: Back to reality

Father, I run to You for strength. I cry to You for peace. Show me how to lay down the financial stress and trust You as we do the best we know to follow Your lead.

April 13, 2001

Dear Lord, I just want to praise and thank You for Your leading. We heard yesterday that we were funded for our grant! [to do on-farm research relating to strawberries] Lord, I trust that You are in this. We prayed that You would close the door if it was not Your will. This opens the door for us to continue on the farm for another year. I claim the promise, "For I know the plans I have for you." I just want to be fully submitted to Your service. "Take me, O Lord, as wholly Thine. I lay all my plans at Thy feet. Use me today in Thy service" (Ellen White, *Steps to Christ*, p. 70).

The strawberries started to bloom. We got busy with the weeding, trusting the Lord for a good harvest. The plants definitely showed the results of not getting them in the ground on time. They were small and immature. Our knowledge was still limited, but we took care of those precious little plants and prayed earnestly that they would still yield a decent crop.

That year we were spared from the normal late spring frosts until April 17 and 18. By then the plants had grown significantly and were looking good. The field had lots of green fruit, and thousands of beautiful little white flowers that promised a good harvest. Still solely dependent on the floating row covers, we knew if it got any colder than 28 degrees, we were in trouble. We started praying that the Lord would send a warm wind to change the forecast. Of course we did our part and covered the berries, fully recognizing how flimsy that protection really was. When we awoke the morning of April 17, we rejoiced that the thermometer registered 43 degrees. God had answered our prayers the first night and sent a fog. We were confident that He would do it again the next. That night we again laid it before the Lord. We went to bed resting and confident the Lord would once more send that warm wind.

Awakening early the next morning, our first thought was the temperature. To our horror, it was 27 degrees! Knowing that the temperatures usually dip just before dawn, we completely understood our predicament. Our hearts sank! There was nothing to do now but go to God's word for peace, comfort, and hope. Together we prayed, knowing that we serve a God who is fully capable of changing even the weather. I was reading my Bible through, and the verses I read that morning could not have been more appropriate! "Grace to you and peace from God our Father, and the Lord Jesus Christ. Blessed be the God and Father of our Lord Jesus Christ, the Father of mercies, and God of all comfort, who comforts us in all our tribulation, that we may be able to comfort those who are in any trouble, with the comfort with which we ourselves are comforted by God" (2 Corinthians 1:2–4).

Over the years these words have been a great solace to us. It was always our prayer that our difficult experiences could help others. We believed that the valleys and hills we traveled were not for our benefit alone. But I did not understand the magnitude of those words on that day. God was preparing me for the deepest valley yet.

From past experience, I had learned it was not good for me to rush out on my own in difficult situations. It is better to wait until John is ready to face reality with me. Walking hand in hand we headed for the field. We dreaded what we might find, and yet we were anxious to look under those covers. With a last prayer for peace, we pulled back the blanket. Before us lay a field of "black-eyed Susans" (the name for dead flowers). We gave up after uncovering only about a third of the field. Our faith was too shaky to speak. We estimated that about 75 percent of the flowers were dead. The ramifications of this were overwhelming. Months of hard work down the drain! John headed to the greenhouse where he watered plants and wrestled with the Lord. I walked home, asking God to give me the face of peace, courage, and faith for the children's sake.

Fortunately, the children were all playing upstairs when I got home. I quietly slipped into the bathroom and splashed cold water on my face, trying to wash away the signs of tears. Sitting on my bed I began folding a load of laundry. My thoughts were centered on our trials. *Lord, Why? How will we survive? What will people say?*

The Scriptures plainly teach us how to have peace (Isaiah 26:3). It never comes by focusing on the trials. While I slogged through the muck and mire of repining, the phone rang. Lifting the receiver I heard the voice of my dear friend Nancy. Immediately I sensed that something was wrong. "Pam, we lost Donald last night." My trials suddenly seemed as nothing. Shock like I had never before experienced hit me in the stomach. My mind raced. "What do you mean you lost him?" I stammered weakly.

Through heart-wrenching sobs Nancy struggled to choke out the words, "He's dead!" My mind and body went numb. We both cried and cried and cried. How could this be!

When she could talk again, Nancy told me that Tom, Donald, Heidi, and a family friend had gone on a canoeing trip the day before. Nancy, along with Tom's parents, walked with them to the starting point, where they prayed for safety. It was a cold morning, so life preservers were donned over jackets, Tom and Heidi led in the first canoe, while Donald and their friend followed. Everyone knew there was a very dangerous set of rapids ahead. They planned to portage around Angel Falls, so they watched intently for the landmarks. But the landmarks were overgrown, so they unknowingly plunged straight into the class five rapids. Both canoes tipped, throwing all occupants and contents into the frigid water. When Tom surfaced downstream he began searching desperately for people, canoes, and belongings. Grabbing floating gear, he called to Heidi; she was okay. Soon the friend appeared. But there was no sign of Donald. "Where's Donald!" was the father's frantic cry. After desperately searching the rapids on their own, Tom raced off to get help. Thus began a day and night of agony for the Hunt family. Search crews combed the river, hoping he had come up farther downstream. There was no sign of him anywhere. Darkness ended the search but it resumed at sunup the next morning. The water levels had dropped overnight and when the search crew went back to the rapids they could see Donald pinned to a large rock in the center of Angel Falls.

Tears streamed down my face as I listened, unbelieving, to this nightmare our friends were going through. How insignificant our problems now seemed! "What can I do to help?" I cried. Nancy assured me they had lots of support. They would let us know when the funeral plans were arranged.

Miraculously, my children's attention was not drawn to my crying in the room below them. They continued their happy play while I slipped out of the house. I blindly stumbled to the greenhouse. John could hear me coming and was there to meet me at the door. It took time for me to sob out the news. We held each other and wept, not only for the Hunt's loss, but also for the loss to our family. In my heart I cried, *Lord, children shouldn't have to face death at such a tender age!* It seemed too much to bear! What would it do to their faith? Trusting that God does not give more than we can bear, we prayed for strength. Hand in hand we trudged home, overwhelmed at the thought of sharing this devastating news with our children.

As we gathered the children, they recognized that something was terribly wrong. The fear in their eyes intensified our pain. It was a time of weeping and heartache such as children should never have to experience. We did all we could to point them to our loving Father who understands our pain. After the crying and endless questions, we talked about our recent visit and all the happy memories we treasured. At the time I thought the children were amazingly resilient. We did not know until years later the depth of the pain our Jonathan suffered. At seven years of age, he had just lost his best friend, but he tried to keep up a brave front.

After sharing with the children, I had an overpowering urge to get in the car and head for the Hunts. Nancy and I were pregnant with Kirsten and Donald at the same time. I was there the day Donald was born. Shouldn't I be there the day he died? I'm not sure what I was thinking, except that I needed to be with her. Stuffing a few things in a bag, I jumped in the car and headed for their home. Emotions are terribly fickle when we are in deep anguish. By the time I got to Nashville, one hour from home, I was overcome with fear of meeting the Hunts alone. I stopped many times and tried to call John, wondering if I should go back home and make plans to go together. But my husband was outside so I could not reach him. Isolated and uncomfortable, but not knowing what else to do, I pressed on.

Arriving on campus, I headed straight to Tom and Nancy's home. It was empty! I soon found the principal who told me they were still at the river. Back at their house, I didn't have long to wait. They crawled out of their car, very surprised to see me. Arms wrapped around each other, we sobbed out our despair and grief. Then I heard the terrible words from Tom, "Where's John?" It was a painful cry from deep inside him, and it compounded my pain. This was no time for me to nurse my own pains. I was there to help and support my friends in any way I could.

Back at home, John finished uncovering our damaged crop. This disaster now seemed like no loss at all. We decided to leave the crop in the Lords hands, and do all in our power to support and serve our friends. Jonathan was heartbroken and unwilling to face his sorrow. He was adamant about the fact that he did not want to go to the funeral. We felt it would be hard to support him while trying to be there for Tom and Nancy, so we decided to leave the boys with my brother's family while Kirsten and John came to the Hunts.

Donald was to be buried in North Carolina, so we travelled there together to make funeral arrangements. The next few days were filled with many intense and intimate moments, from picking out the casket, to making plans for the service. We had many heart-to-heart conversations and prayers. Many times we grieved together in silence. All of us chose to put our trust in God.

The Lord gave John a beautiful message of hope and comfort for the funeral service. Tom shared from his heart that if one person came to know Christ through the death of his son, he would count it worth the loss. In the valley of death, Tom and Nancy found comfort in Jesus, and through their faith and trust in God, many were blessed. Together with family and friends, we laid that faithful, young soldier of the cross to rest, where he "sleeps" until Jesus calls him forth to everlasting life. With great longing we look forward to that day, and until then, we remind ourselves, "The *best* is yet to come!"

Back at the farm after Donald's funeral, we stepped straight into spring. There were ripe strawberries in the field! The frost that killed the flowers did not damage the green fruit that had already set. We guessed that the crop would start normally, then have a lull because of the blooms lost to the frost. We hoped for more fruit at the end of the season from flowers that had not yet bloomed. In the *Berry Bulletin* (a publication John put together each spring), he summed it up this way:

It's been another busy year at Bountiful Blessings Organic Farm. It often seems as if we are taking one step forward and two steps back, but we are learning and growing and slowly working toward our goal of a real, working farm! We feel truly blessed, and praise the Lord (our Senior Partner) for His leading.

We are so thankful for the blessings of life, health, strength, and a beautiful country setting to live and work in. When this farming business gets a little discouraging, we remind ourselves that this is what the Lord led us to do, and He has a plan to bless us—no matter what the weather does!

It was no stellar crop, to be sure. The lateness of the fall planting, and the losses in the spring took their toll. We did the best we could with what we had, and soon our third crop was behind us. Our faith and courage were still intact in spite of the challenges. Our commitment and call to serve were confirmed, and we were determined to shoulder with peace and joy the trials the Lord allowed. As soon as one crop was finished, our sights were set on the next one. We felt confident that next year would surely be better!

CHAPTER 8

Our Long Winter

SUMMER 2001–SPRING 2002

Sitting our little ones, who were six, eight, and nine on the couch, John said, "Children, do you remember Laura Ingalls' book *The Long Winter?*"

"Oh yes!" they chorused, "That was one of our favorites."

John was great at building excitement and enthusiasm! "Well, guess what?" he paused for effect and the children sat wide-eyed on the edge of the couch, their little feet dangling far from the floor, "We are going to have our very own Long Winter!"

Up to this time we had shielded our children from much of the "privation" that dogged our new life. But they were getting older and becoming more aware. The coming winter promised to be more challenging than anything we'd faced so far. Our young ones were such troopers! They did not complain or make us feel bad about living without many things that others had. We felt confident they would accept and understand our situation.

We explained that the strawberry crop had not provided enough money to meet our needs. The children understood that the markets were not very profitable that summer. They also knew that John's work at the neighbor's had ended. As a result, there was very little money to go around. Because we lived near several extended family members, we needed to use special care to keep our adventure a secret. We coached the children on behavior at Grandma and Grandpa's house. We all chose to be careful not to talk about things we didn't have at our house, like peanut butter and jelly. It would be our secret. We explained that God wanted us to bear our little trials with a happy attitude. Our precious youngsters embraced this new experience and never once breathed a word to anyone!

Our choice to keep the details a secret from our family may seem strange to some, but we had voluntarily quit our jobs and we felt it would be wrong to go out looking for sympathy and asking for hand-outs. We chose this life in answer to God's call. He allowed the trials. He had lessons to teach us, and we were not looking for an escape route. We embraced it as His Individualized Educational Plan (IEP) for the John Dysinger family. We were confident in the Lord's leading. We knew there were more lessons for us to learn, and that these lessons would shape our characters, our vision, and our family

In June each year, after the strawberry season was finished, John took a day with the Lord to ask for continued direction. Usually John was impressed that he had lost some of his focus on serving. It was very easy to let his time be completely consumed with making the farm a financial success. The business of farming was not to be our focus. We did not want to forget why God had called us to this business in the first place. God continued to impress both of us that we were exactly where He wanted us to be, doing just what He called us to do. God placed man in a garden in the beginning. Man has since devised many occupations and lifestyles, but we believe that nothing has improved upon the original plan. Despite the obstacles, God had not changed His mind about our calling to farm.

Sweetness in life

Kirsten reached an exciting milestone that summer. She had made and sold granola for about two years, and saved her pennies carefully towards the purchase of her very own dog. Now she had enough! August 11, 2001 was the appointed day to look at puppies. We asked God to go before us and to give discernment in finding just the right one. We asked Him to help us find the puppy quickly too, because we didn't have much time to devote to the search. Grandma volunteered to keep the boys while Kirsten, John, and I arranged to see three different poodle litters.

The first two stops left us empty-handed We started to wonder if we would go home without a puppy that day. Kirsten didn't want to be unreasonable, but she did want to be confident that she had made the right choice. At our last stop we met Kirsten's dog! She was the tiniest, cutest, most rambunctious little curly-haired poodle we had ever seen! It was love at first sight! We watched her, played with her, and felt sure she was the one for us. Kirsten handed over her hard-earned money and became the proud owner of a toy poodle. We did not forget to thank the Lord for answering our prayers.

Kirsten has always been into names, so it is amazing that she did not have a list all made up from which to choose. After much thought, she decided on the name Sugar, in honor of the sweetest part of her granola recipe! For the next thirteen years, Sugar remained a five-pound bundle of energy. She blessed our lives with much fun, love, laughter, and sweetness.

Not long after getting Sugar, we propagated another batch of strawberry plants. The process was getting easier with the experience gained from each passing year. This year we determined to get everything done on time. The previous year's late start taught us the vital lesson that we must do whatever it takes to stay on the correct planting schedule.

As usual, the financial stresses were intense. I struggled with mixed feelings and felt my inadequacy as the manager of our meager funds.

September 13, 2001

Our bank account is overdrawn! I have no laundry soap and no oil—these are the most urgent needs. John will not be working at the neighbors this winter because she has hired someone full time. The garden produce is about gone. The greenhouse is full of strawberry plants waiting to be planted, so we can't plant lettuce in there. I am like a child away at school and writing home to say, "Father, please send money!"

We are doing our best to follow Your lead, but feel like we have made a mess. Trusting You to help us sort it out!

God did help us. We sold some strawberry plants and found twenty dollars from a previous market day. This got us by for a short moment. The Long Winter had begun and it wasn't even winter yet!

October 23, 2001

Heavenly Father, we have hit a low in staple items, yet I have peace. Thank You! When I don't have oil or salt it makes it hard, but we can manage for a while. Usually when we are out of oil we find a few dollars to get some. The list of staple items we are out of is long, but I praise You for peace and also for providing a way to get them. I am selling a box of walnuts that I got so I can go to the store with $50—which will get me all I need. Thank You, Father for the lessons we are learning that are far more valuable than monetary gain. My only desire is to live abiding in You.

We asked some friends to come visit during our "long winter adventure." They had no idea that they were eating our very last rice and beans. The reason we invited them over was to get some counsel. We asked them some philosophical questions about faith and works. We needed a better understanding of what part is God's, and what part is ours. We were desperately trying to find the balance. We knew that most people would tell us we were totally out of balance. We respected our guests as a couple who had years of experience and wisdom. They were people who lived by faith and always put the kingdom of Heaven first in their lives. Of course we did not tell them everything that was going on. We were looking for principles that applied in our situation. When they left that day, we were at peace. We had renewed confidence we were doing all God had impressed us to do. We could rest in confidence, knowing that He would provide.

November 6, 2001

I am excited about the peace I feel in my heart. We have never been financially tighter. . . . The food supply is getting low . . . but I'm peaceful! Clothing is wearing out . . . but I'm at peace. Through your strength, I am coming to truly embrace this as Your plan for us. I realize that "poverty" is a blessing and has enabled us to live a quiet, simple life. . . . May we never resent or question your leading. Keep us where we are . . . doing what we are doing . . . struggling if we need to . . . until we have learned to trust You!

That evening John and I had one of those extra-special prayer times that stay in memory's halls. We grappled with the fact that we were not making it financially. We simply did not know how to proceed, so we turned to the Lord and cried out to Him.

After putting the children to bed, John turned to me and said, "I'm going to seek the Lord." I was concerned about my burdened husband. All he longed to do was stay in the Lord's will. Why was it so hard? We knelt to pray, pleading for understanding and direction. The burdens were so heavy on John that I felt sure he would return home with answers. As he opened the door, a cold blast of air hit me. Quickly he slid out and the door closed behind him. I was alone—yet not alone. Our magnificent Creator God would be both with my husband, as he walked the hills and valleys of the farm, and with me to comfort and encourage. I was determined to pray for John until he returned home. Later, I was awakened from my sleep as the door opened and John crept in. Groggily I looked at the clock and was relieved that it wasn't later. "So what is the word?" I asked anxiously. Here's John's story in his own words:

As I left the house and headed toward the pond, it felt as if a literal weight was bearing down on my shoulders. The burdens of life were trying to crush me. Here I was, the husband and "provider" having totally failed, it seemed, to take care of my family. I was willing to do anything, but was committed to "lean not on my own understanding" (Proverbs 3:5). All I wanted was a word from the Lord. I wanted *Him* to "direct my paths" (vs 6). Was that too much to ask?

Stumbling along, I cried out to the Lord, "Please just give me some direction and assurance. I can't continue like this unless I know we are still in Your will. 'I will not let You go unless You bless me' (Genesis 32:26). Please Lord, I beg of You some assurance of Your love and continued guidance. I'm not going home until I'm confident You are still in control."

By this time, I had arrived at the pond. It was a cold, clear, moonless night. Like Abraham of old, I looked up at the countless stars. Reaching out my tiny hand of faith, I attempted to place it in the hand of an Omnipotent God. He had said He would never leave us or forsake us (Hebrews 13:5). Could I take Him at his word? Like Jacob, I felt I was wrestling with God. Could I trust Him or not?

As I stood on the dam, gazing up into the starry sky, all of a sudden the sky lit up like lightning. Instinctively, I turned around in time to see a huge fireball of flaming color slowly descending over the hill—leaving a glowing trail behind it. Chills ran down my spine and the hair on the back of my neck stood up. I felt I was standing on holy ground. "Thank You, Lord," I whispered. "It is enough. I can press on now." I headed home with lightened step and a heart full of praise to a God who cared enough about "little old me" to give me reassurance of His love.

As I slid into bed, Pam asked, "What is the word?"

"Press on," I said, "God is still with us!"

ASKING FOR SIGNS

People seem a little nervous about asking God for signs. It seems risky—especially knowing that "false Christs" and "false prophets" will use signs and wonders to deceive in the last days (Matthew 24:24).

Yes, it would be very risky if you *based* your decisions on signs. Your future should be guided by a "thus saith the Lord" from His Word. But, there is ample evidence in the Bible that God often *confirms* His Word through signs.

Consider Gideon: an angel of the Lord came to Him with clear directions, but Gideon asked for signs of confirmation not once, not twice, not . . . Well, you figure out how many times for yourself in Judges 6,7.

It's interesting that, in Genesis 1:14, God says the lights in the heavens are to be for *signs* and seasons. I was unfamiliar with this text until long after the Lord sent me a sign in the heavens to comfort and confirm.

Would He like us to trust Him without having to use signs and wonders? Probably (see John 4:48). But, He is so compassionate and long-suffering with us! He remembers that we are dust (Psalm 103:14), and is willing to go above and beyond to show us His love.

By November 25, John and I felt that we needed to re-calculate what our financial needs really were. Adding up all of our bills that were past due or soon to be due was a bit depressing. The sum total was $1,296.94! That was a tremendous amount of money for us. Daily we were laying our needs before the Lord and looking for His guidance to show us how to remedy our situation. Yet the only peace we found was in doing our best with the work before us on the farm.

My courage was always best in the morning. I came forth from my time alone with Jesus strengthened to face the trials of the day. The day before Thanksgiving, there was a knock on the front door. Peering through the window, I saw a man standing on the porch. When I opened the door I could see he was from the electric company. Kindly, he stated he was there to either collect payment or turn our power off. I was not surprised; we were way overdue in paying the bill. Quickly a verse from the Bible popped into my mind, "before they call, I will answer" (Isaiah 65:24). Just the night before, I had taught my first piano lesson with a neighbor. She insisted on paying me, not just for the first lesson, or for the first month, but for two months in advance. This provided just enough money to keep them from turning off our power! Praise God! With rejoicing in my heart, I ran out to where John was working on the tractor and told him how the Lord had provided for us.

A memorable Thanksgiving

"Come, Ye Thankful People, Come." I longed to be one of those thankful people but it wasn't easy. We always tried to be a blessing to others on the holidays. For several years we dressed our children as pilgrims and Indians, and went with my brother's family to the hospital to sing to the patients. It was a sure way to lift my spirits. Bringing joy to others always brings joy to oneself! After this year's trip to the hospital we headed home to enjoy a very simple Thanksgiving dinner.

That evening we accepted an invitation to an extended-family bonfire. At that time we found it hard to attend such gatherings, because we felt rather out of place with our well-to-do relatives. But the Lord impressed us to go, so we went. Before leaving the house, I remembered that I wanted to give *We Would See Jesus* to one of the family members. I grabbed that book from the shelf in our bedroom. As I did so, I felt impressed to take another book by the same author. The title of the second book was *The Calvary Road*. I argued with the impression, but just in case it was the Lord's idea, I stuffed both of the books in my pocket. Then we hurriedly left the house.

In spite of my misgivings, it was good to see family and we enjoyed our visit. Before leaving, I told the family member I had a book for her. As I gave it to her, she called her brother over. "Isn't this the book you were just telling me you wanted to get?" she asked.

The brother took the book in his hands with a surprised look on his face. "It's the same author," he said, "but the one I want is called *The Calvary Road*."

At that moment, I knew why I had *The Calvary Road* in my pocket. Pulling it out, I said, "The Lord must have wanted you to have this today." We were both dumbfounded! How could it be that I, being at an all-time low financially, could give a gift to someone who has more money than I will see in my lifetime? It was because I was learning to listen to the Lord. His still, small voice had impressed me to bring that book—giving me, the person with "nothing," the opportunity to bless someone who had "everything!" It was as if the Lord was saying, *"Remember, it's not about money."*

Our situation got more desperate and John started taking more and more time alone with the Lord. We put together some gift baskets with farm goodies and soaps that I had made. John and the children went out and tried to sell them but the results were dismal! I took a bunch of the baskets and home-made body products to a craft fair. This required lots of work. I had to create a nice presentation, pack it all in the car, haul it in to the fair booth, set it up, spend a long day there, take it down, haul it back to the car. I struggled to get the leftovers back into the house, and finally, I had to put it all away. All that for a measly twenty-six dollars!

I felt like everything we tried was a financial failure. John applied for holiday work at UPS. Immediately, we both felt a loss of peace. Were we trying to take our future into our own hands? There was plenty of work to do on the farm, so it was hard to think of John going away to work. But we were clearly in a desperate situation. John was willing to do anything—as long as he knew God was leading. From our study of the Scriptures we believed that clear guidance from the Lord was not too much to ask. We continued in prayer, seeking the Lord, and thanking Him for the peace He was giving.

December 3, 2001

Father, John, like Jacob, wants to be with You until he has the answer. Should I expect him back in a few hours or a few days? It's kind of exciting to know that when I see him next, he will have a word from You. Our only desire is to do Your will!

John returned home at midnight saying he'd decided the Lord was not going to give any answers now. The only answer was "I Am all you need!"

On December 7, I had the opportunity to visit with a lovely Christian mom who lives in our area. I'll call her Alice. Alice was a trusted friend with whom I could talk quite freely about our situation. Her family was also on a faith journey, so she could understand our commitment to following God. We prayed together, and I shared with her some of our experience. She prayed that the Lord would in some way encourage us. I felt *she* was the answer to her own prayer! It was so refreshing to share with someone openly about how things were going.

I testified that God was sustaining and giving us peace amid the trials. Because their family had also experienced very difficult times, Alice was able, with confidence, to encourage me that God had a plan and that He would not let us down.

Unexpected letter

At this time we did not have a bank mortgage on our home. Two individuals had offered personal loans to help finance the building of our cabin. We made regular monthly payments to one of those parties until October, when money became extremely tight. At the end of November, John wrote to this individual asking if we could suspend our monthly payments until spring when we believed that finances would improve so that we could resume payments.

The day after my visit with Alice we received an unexpected letter from our creditor. To our shock, the letter stated that we could suspend the monthly payments until we were able to continue. More than this, it said that there would be no hard feelings if we were unable to pay at all. A wave of relief rolled over us.

Then, there was a hand-written P.S.:

"I have decided we would forgive your debt to us—please consider your debt paid in full. When and if you are doing well in the future it would be nice if you would do something nice for someone else."

We were overwhelmed! The Lord was so merciful and we felt so undeserving. What a blessing! This news was incredible. It did not, however, change the fact that our pantry was empty! I continued to pray for peace amid the privation, and God gave it to me.

December 23, 2001

Father, You have showed me perfect peace as I look to Jesus and changeable peace as I focus on circumstances.

January 1, 2002

Father, this has probably been the most difficult year of my life! But we all have our health, so really how difficult has it been? . . . It was a year of financial stress, the

95

worst I've ever known. In the spring we had a 30 percent yield of strawberries. We've nearly had our power turned off and phone disconnected. Because of not paying the bill on time, our credit card interest rate went up to 25 percent. There has been no money for food for the last three months. We haven't had granola for weeks! Tomato soup and popcorn have been our staples, but the amazing thing is no one has complained; . . . the children are maturing and growing in You. They are content with very little and have a very generous spirit. This year we decided to give a third-world family a llama for our family Christmas. We were given a gift of cash for the exact amount needed. Our children had such a giving spirit even though they knew there would be little or nothing for them. In fact, we haven't even given them their gifts yet, and what we have is very small (but they're happy). It takes so little to cheer their hearts. I can see Your hand at work in their lives. I thank You and praise You for that.

Over the holidays, the financial pressures lessened a bit. We sold quite a few gift baskets after all and John did a few odd jobs that helped us get through. In February, John and I made a trip to North Carolina to attend a Strawberry Growers convention. We came home with an abundance of ideas and with courage to press on. John had attended a frost protection workshop. He was sure we needed to have a pump and sprinkler system this year. The losses we sustained during the last two seasons would have paid for *many* pumps and sprinklers. How we secured the money for the system, I don't remember. I imagine we used our credit card. We did not use credit cards to live on but we occasionally used them for farm purchases. The spring frosts were still ahead of us and we were determined to do everything in our power to protect the crop. We had used the row covers and prayer but had suffered much loss. This year was going to be different!

Spring frost saga

One of the most difficult parts of growing strawberries is getting them through the unpredictable spring weather. Between rain and frost, it can be a challenge. Character is built in many ways, but I'm convinced frost protection, even with a sprinkler system, is up there at the top of the list. The first step is covering the plants with floating row covers early enough in the day to trap a little heat. Dozens of times we failed to meet that deadline. Then we would all be out there tugging and pulling on cold, and sometimes frozen covers. After the covers are on, you monitor the temperature—which means a lot of getting up and checking. In later years we got an alarm system to get us up when there was actual danger.

When the temperature dips to near 32 degrees under the covers, you turn the sprinklers on. Now, if that was the end of the job it wouldn't be so bad, but the worst is still to come. Some growers stay up all night—walking the fields to make sure the sprinklers don't get clogged. We chose a more temperate route with more reliable sprinklers. Every hour or two John would groggily crawl out of bed, pull on his coveralls, open the front door, wake up with a blast of cold air, and head to the field. Quickly, he would make the rounds of the field with a flashlight checking to make sure everything was functioning properly. Inevitably there would be one or two sprinklers stuck. This necessitated venturing into the field to unstick them. He had to walk up and down the aisles of that icy field and knock the sprinklers to get them wobbling again. While walking in the field, freezing water sometimes hit him in the face. His coveralls became caked with ice. Through all of that he had to work hard to keep from slipping on the frozen covers.

Just imagine doing frost detail multiple times in a night, and then several nights in a row. That is just what was happening the first week in April. John had frost-protected three nights in a row. On Sabbath, April 6, we went to see some friends who had moved away from our area and were back for a visit. Catching up on one another's lives meant talking about the farm and how things were going for us. John shared about the losses of previous crops due to the frost damage. He told how the Lord was blessing this year, and that we had not yet sustained any loss.

I am ashamed to admit my thoughts, but I must in order for you to understand the immensity of the message the Lord was about to send to me. My thoughts were something like this: *The Lord? You mean the pump!* Looking back it is clear that I was harboring some bitterness against the Lord for the failure of previous crops. When John gave the Lord the credit, my heart was saying, *It's not the Lord, it's the pump!* Oh how little I really knew the ways of the Almighty. One thing I was about to learn. His compassion never fails.

Frost protecting is a real science. One thing that was drilled into John's memory at the workshop was, "once you turn the sprinklers on it is CRITICAL that the flow of water not stop." This constant application of water freezes on the plants, flowers, and berries, but as water freezes it releases heat and keeps the temperature of the plant above 32 degrees. It is an amazing sight to see the field covered with a thick layer of ice. When the sun melts away the ice, an unharmed crop is left, basking in the morning warmth.

Back to April 6: We arrived at home late. We had to pull the covers on in the cold and dark. We wondered how much good they would do, but we were determined to do our part. After finishing the job we prayed for the Lord's protection and headed home. John calculated how quickly the temperature was dropping and decided to get up at midnight. By then the temperature was nearing 32 degrees so he fired up the pump and turned on the sprinklers. He got up again at 2 a.m. and intended to get up at 4, but we both slept soundly through the alarm. I awoke with a start at 5 a.m. Realizing that John had missed the 4 a.m. rounds, I quickly woke him up. He rolled out of bed with a groan, pulling on his soggy coveralls. Walking to the door, he opened it and stepped onto the porch.

The terrifying sound of silence met his ears! Why was it silent? Why couldn't he hear the pump? Slamming the door, he ran to the pump. Remembering the frost protection seminar, he knew that without a miracle the crop was frozen solid. There was no use figuring out what was wrong with the pump. At this point it would be worse to turn it back on than to just leave it off. Slowly he trudged home. Coming to my side of the bed, he knelt down and said, "Honey, the pump has stopped. We have to pray for mercy."

Falling to our knees, we felt our total dependency on our Heavenly Father. We prayed earnestly that the Lord would spare our crop—promising that we would give Him all the praise and glory if He worked a miracle. Journaling is therapy for me, so taking my pencil I poured out my heart to the Lord.

April 7, 2002

Father, Forgive Me! I realize that even though we are using this frost protecting equipment, You are still the only One we can trust. I thank You for this reminder . . . reality check. . . . Nothing in this world functions without Your watch care, not even pumps. Let us never forget this. . . . But now we throw ourselves into Your loving arms asking for mercy. Heavenly Father, please don't let us lose the crop . . . but most of all give us peace and comfort. We choose to trust You to do for us what You see best.

The sun rose, melting the icy field. Once again John and I walked hand in hand to the strawberry field. Our hearts were pounding. With much fear and trepidation we began to lift the covers. Memories of last year's loss were still raw. We cringed at the thought of going through that again. Slowly, we lifted the corner. With unbelieving eyes we gazed upon our crop—completely untouched by the frost! Tears of joy washed down our faces as our eyes feasted on the mercy of the Lord. He, in His love and tenderness toward us, His erring children, had performed an undeniable miracle, and saved the whole crop! We could not contain the joy and thankfulness that flooded our souls. Running home, we gathered the children together and had a session of praise and thanksgiving for God's mercies! But God wasn't finished giving us a testimony to share about that crop.

April 17, 2002

Last night we awoke with a start to pounding rain and hail. Kirsten also woke up and together we fell on our knees and cried out to the Lord to protect our crop. I freely admit, and You know, I didn't have perfect peace in my heart. But I, like the disciples of long ago, turned to You. You are my refuge and strength, my ever present help in trouble. Now it is calm and the environment is at peace. . . . You have given me calmness in my heart that is deeper than the external results of last night.

Sometimes the Lord says yes . . . sometimes no. That night we experienced, once again, one of His yes moments! There was no sign of hail damage to the crop. Another miracle! Our hearts went out to a grower just thirty minutes from us whose crop was so badly damaged that he never even opened his strawberry patch that season. Why him and not us? I can't say. What I can say is that we serve the living God, the Creator of all. Our life goal is to love and trust Him so completely that we will be unshaken in that trust no matter what happens. We knew God has a purpose in all that He allows.

The 2002 strawberry crop went on to do beautifully and we shared freely how the success was twice over a miracle.

Our Long Winter came to an end. Our faith had been stretched. God's faithfulness had been felt. Lessons were learned, and character developed. With courage, we made plans for our next crop, hoping that the hardest experiences were behind us.

CHAPTER 9

The Year of Investment

SUMMER 2002–SPRING 2003

"To all who are reaching out to feel the guiding hand of God, the moment of greatest discouragement is the time when Divine help is nearest. They will look back with thankfulness upon the darkest part of their way. . . . From every temptation and every trial He will bring them forth with firmer faith." (Ellen White, *The Desire of Ages*, p. 528).

The more desperate the situation, the more glorious will be the deliverance. The question is, where is your focus when the trial hits? Are you looking to the arm of flesh for your deliverance or are you on your knees pleading for the mercy of the Lord? When things don't turn out as you think they should, are you blaming God, yourself, others? Or are you saying, "Father, what can You teach me from this situation? How can I learn to trust You more through it?" If we are seeking God with all our hearts, then we must accept the challenges as coming through His hands for the purpose of strengthening our faith and trust.

The first days of July found us full of the hustle and bustle that always accompanies deadlines. We were invited to have a booth at a local Fourth-of-July festival. This was the first time we had done anything like this, but we believed it would give us opportunity to make more contacts in the community. Consenting to participate was the easy part; getting ready was a lot of work. The children and I made jam, bottled honey, rolled beeswax candles, and wrapped and labeled soap, lip balms, and body butters (this was a side business I had started in my "free" time). There were signs and brochures to print and a display to design and construct. Kirsten, at ten, was an amazing helper, and the boys willingly did anything they could. We spent long hours getting ready for this event, and prayed that the Lord would make our family a blessing. Of course we hoped to make some money, but getting to know people was in the forefront of our thinking.

July fourth dawned sunny and warm. Packing the children into the car, we headed for the fairgrounds. There was lots of activity as the various exhibitors set up their displays. The children were animated and thoroughly enjoyed the excitement. We gave them various jobs at the booth. While Joshua played quietly with cars and trucks, Jonathan handed out brochures, and Kirsten asked one question—"Would you be interested in organic strawberries next spring?" That got us their contact information every time!

It was a great day and we met many interesting people, but one couple stands out above the crowd. They were young, with two adorable little children. Casually stopping by our table they looked at the various items we offered. Their questions about the farm gave us the perfect opportunity to share how God had led our family. It was easy to see their interest in our story. Soon we turned the question around and asked about their family. To our surprise, they shared a more dramatic countercultural move than we had made. Burned out by the fast pace of life, these two physicians had both quit their jobs and come home to be a family. Of course there was an instant bond between us. Little did we know that the Lord would use that bond to bless us in a devastating time of need.

On Jonathan's birthday we gave him a gift with this riddle on the top: "What grows in the dark and lives in the light?" The children were stumped and gave up so we said, "If you open the gift, you may get a hint." Out tumbled blue and pink baby clothes. Shouts of joy and unbelief followed. Jonathan jumped onto my lap and hugged me with joy. Yes, we had all longed to add to our family, but the farm had been so intense and draining. Now we thought we had turned the corner and things were looking up. It was the perfect time to extend our family. What a blessing that we didn't know the future!

We also presented Jonathan with a box that was noisy. Besides that, it was moving around on the floor. His nine-year-old eyes were full of curiosity. As he opened the lid, out hopped two of the cutest lop-eared rabbits. In Kirsten's mind, the first order of business was naming them. She worked with Jonathan who gladly consented to his sister's preferences; Peter and Molly it was! We built cages, purchased water bottles and food, and Jonathan's rabbit business was established! This little business would teach him responsibility, care of animals, money management, and many other life skills—at least that was the hope.

Finances continued to be a major stressor. There was not enough money to run the farm *and* expand it to meet our needs. How do you build a business when you don't have money? It takes money to make money! God had just spared our crop in such a miraculous way. We rationalized that we should be more confident in taking a risk, knowing that He was leading us. Wouldn't He want us to invest in the farm? Wouldn't He bless it? We did what seemed to make the most "business sense" (not that John and I had much of that). We mortgaged our house.

Part of our plan with the mortgage money was to expand our strawberry operation. Preparations were made to plant one and a half acres—twenty-four thousand plants, to be exact. Our idealism about not using plastic was gone, so we invested in woven landscape fabric (so we could re-use it for many years—our compromise with plastic), and John laboriously burned twenty-four thousand holes in it. We were still making all our own potting mix and hand blocking a dozen at a time. The job could have been overwhelming, but our children, on whom we depended at every stage, were becoming excellent help. It was a family affair. All hands had to get dirty, and learn to do so without complaining. My father had become an integral part of our operation. He faithfully came each August while we were propagating. He came again in September for planting, and in the spring for delivering berries. We needed him and he needed us.

That year we determined once again to do everything right! The strawberries were propagated on time, planted on time, and regularly sprayed. We did all in our power to ensure a bumper harvest in the spring.

John, like most farmers, is great at calculating, speculating, and forecasting. His journals are full of numbers and projections. He figured if we got "average" yields (he always tried to be conservative in calculating), we could pay our loan off in a couple of years. We were so confident in God's leading and blessing in the past (especially the sparing of our crop and the forgiving of our debt) that we didn't even ask ourselves the question, "what if . . . ?"

Thanksgiving that year was a time of peace and joy. John and I both felt it!

Thanksgiving, 2002

Dear Lord, on this day of Thanksgiving, I want to reflect on Your goodness to me, and all that I have to be thankful for. . . . Thank You for leading us to farming. It hasn't been easy, but it's been so good for building faith, and learning lessons of industry and perseverance. Thank You for the trials which have taught us that You are all we need.

Thanksgiving, 2002

"I will sing to the Lord, because He has dealt bountifully with me." Father, that is the deepest feeling in my heart. You have dealt bountifully with me! I thank You for every way You have shown me that bounty.

Investing in our farm

For the first three years of farming, we ran the strawberry business from our front porch. Customers came to the house to get picking trays. We sent them off to the field to pick, and when they were done they would return to the house to pay. If they needed water or a bathroom, we sent them to our house, whether we were there or not. This made many people uncomfortable, even though we did our best to make them feel welcome. The third year we managed to pour a concrete slab in a portion of the old tobacco barn which sat at the top end of the fields. This gave us a place to keep all the picking containers, but it didn't fix our bathroom needs.

Looking back, we see it was probably a mistake to take out the mortgage, but we also made mistakes in deciding how to use the money. We used a portion of the money to put a bathroom and a store in the barn. We added a large front porch with rockers onto the barn, and picnic tables to encourage customers to bring a lunch and enjoy a day in the country. It may seem a little crazy, but at this point we were trying to have a huge spring push and earn most of our money for the year. For many of our customers, coming to the farm was a family affair. While parents picked strawberries, the children played in the creeks. For a few short hours, the young ones had a chance to enjoy the life of a country kid. These were all valuable additions to our farm, but none of them directly improved our financial picture.

In addition to making the barn more functional, we put in a three-thousand-foot long, four-inch wide water line from the pond to the strawberry patch. This gave us an amazing gravity flow irrigation system. No more need for the pump! We put a heater in the greenhouse in hopes of getting early tomatoes, and purchased an expensive spading machine for our tractor. We felt that all of these things would make our farm more profitable the following spring.

January

Heavenly Father, we have reason to hope that this year our farm will become a viable operation. Our plants have never looked better! We have invested a lot of money in farm improvements and we pray that You will bless our efforts. I feel great peace about the farm and thank You for Your leading.

Oh how short lived that feeling of peace was!

The funds for the farm have run out! We have not finished the barn. The propane went three times faster than we imagined. What we anticipated would last the season is gone in only three weeks! The strawberries are full of weeds, but it's been raining for a solid week. We have to borrow more money to finish up the projects. We had committed not to do that, but what do we do? We desperately need help but we can't afford it. But we also can't afford not to have help. I realize we have made many mistakes. This grieves me because we have truly tried to follow Your leading. . . . I'm overwhelmed!

John had his own struggles with being overwhelmed and losing focus.

========================= **February 9, 2003** =========================
And there's the farm . . . You know how consuming are the thoughts—and the energies. I don't feel like I have time for anything other than the farm . . . but what to do?

========================= **February 13, 2003** =========================
Dear Lord, this morning I've been impressed with the fact that I've lost my focus. I left teaching to lead my family to Heaven, and now I'm focused on making the farm a success.

Lord, please save me from myself. . . . I don't want to be focused on things of this world!

========================= **March 2, 2003** =========================
Why is it that I get so caught up in the future of the farm? I want to be a diligent, industrious worker, but I don't want my thoughts and energies consumed by the farm.

After much prayer we decided to do whatever it took to have a good spring crop. That meant hiring people to help us with the weeding and other work that was beyond what we could possibly do. We added credit card debt to our mortgage and tried to remain confident that the Lord was going to bless our efforts. We anticipated being bountifully repaid in May. No one could accuse us of not doing our part! We worked incredibly long hours. The loft of our house was full of tender little plants waiting to be moved to the greenhouse.

As spring approached, we had our greenhouse FULL of bedding plants—both flowers and vegetables. Stationed in front of each variety was a beautifully laminated color picture with descriptions and growing directions. Large coco fiber baskets hung from all the rafters of the greenhouse, promising that by Mother's Day there would be beautifully colored flowers cascading over their rims. The farm store was decorated and full of jams, honey, candles, soaps, and many other hand-crafted items. We had a "create-your-own gift" center with bags, tissue, and all kinds of "farmy" gift items. The freezer was full of "Joshua's Juice Pops," Jonathan had perfected his "Cookies for Keys" (piano lesson fund), and "Kirsten's Krunchy Granola" was in place to meet all the demands we knew would come! The porch was bedecked with rockers and a glider where customers could sit and sip strawberry lemonade. They would be invited to bring their lunch and enjoy one of the picnic tables placed near the gurgling brook.

Spring frost

Frost protecting went smoothly that year. Although John had several all-nighters, the crop looked amazing! We also had some close calls with hail. Learning from the previous year's experience, we didn't put too much trust in the equipment. Instead, we went to our knees—asking the Lord to keep things running smoothly. There was more at stake than ever before. We had given it all the business savvy we had. Our debt was modest, from a business debt point of view, but we had the additional credit card debt from hiring laborers to finish the work we started. Nevertheless, we were confident the crop would be blessed, and we would pay off a fair chunk of it that spring. Peace reigned in our hearts knowing that between the store, the greenhouse, the spring crops, and the strawberries, we would be rewarded for all our hard work. We were poised for success!

Having accomplished all of my goals, I sat back peacefully and awaited the arrival of our fourth child. April 4, 2003 dawned warm and sunny—the picture-perfect spring day! I knew our baby would arrive that day. This time we had a midwife and planned a home birth. As contractions increased, I sent word to John that he should come home, but he was busy trying to give our worker (who didn't speak English) a full day's worth of work. He did not realize the urgency of my situation. I brought the children into my room and told them, "The day we've been waiting for is finally here—*today* you will hold your baby brother or sister." My parents and Nana were with us. When Dad heard that I was in labor he came in and offered a beautiful and comforting prayer.

By 10 a.m. I was very anxious because John had not yet arrived. Calling Kirsten, I sent an urgent SOS to him. My precious mother, who has no medical background, set everything out in preparation for the birth. She is always calm under pressure, but I imagine she was a bit stressed about the fact that there was no father and no midwife present! John rushed in the door and a sense of relief swept over me as he assured me that everything was going to be all right. That's my husband! Calm and steady at the most intense moments. The midwife arrived at 10:40, and Caleb John Dysinger was born at 10:50! Kirsten sat by my side as my mother announced, "Just what every farmer needs—another son!"

Before my parents headed for home, my father took John for a little walk down to the strawberry field. Dad's hand swept across the field as he said, "John, look at all those berries!" They were green at this point and the plants were covered with flowers. A casual counting told us that most plants had over forty fruits or blooms, which for us was amazing. I can just hear my father, with a chuckle of joy in his voice say, "John, what are you going to do with them all?"

Nothing is ever a surprise to the Lord and more than that, He answers before we call (Isaiah 65:24). Two years earlier, God paved the way for this challenge. While selling at a local farmers' market, a reporter from the *Tennessean*—the Greater Nashville newspaper—introduced herself to John, telling him, "If you're ever interested in having an article on your farm just let me know." This was the time! We contacted the reporter and she was happy to make an appointment for an interview near the end of April. She brought a photographer and we had a wonderful time sharing God's leading on the farm. Before leaving, she added that she couldn't promise they would run the article, and if they did, she didn't know when it would be. All we could do was trust in God's timing.

April 30, two days after our interview, the phone started ringing at six o'clock in the morning. Yes, the article had come out! I spent most of the day on the phone answering a multitude of questions. The next day was to be our season opener, and it promised to be a fantastic first day. Despite the article saying we opened at nine in the morning, the first car drove onto the farm at seven! John made his way to the field while I tried to get the children fed and out the door. Everyone had his part to play. Kirsten managed the greenhouse, John supervised the strawberry and vegetable fields, the boys picked berries, my father-in-law directed traffic, my mother-in-law provided lunch, and I managed the store. Caleb's main job was to sleep in a little room near the cash register while I checked people out and helped them with their berries. At the end of the day we dropped, exhausted but excited. We had made $2,000 and we hadn't even picked half of the field!

Sunday, May 4, 2003, was the most amazing day our farm has ever seen. We all occupied the same posts as the previous picking day. The only difference was the volume of traffic. The field was full of pickers, people sat on the porch enjoying strawberry lemonade, Joshua's Juice Pops dripped down the faces of precious children, visitors to the greenhouse were awed by our little vegetable and flower "specialist," children played in the creek, and hundreds of pounds of berries left the field. I spent my day behind the cash register where lines of people waited to check out. As the day came to an end, we were exhausted and exhilarated. We had made $3,500 dollars in one day! With only two days behind us, we were well on the way to reaching our crop goals! We still hadn't picked the whole field, which was becoming a concern: overripe berries can spoil the maturing fruit and spread disease.

That night when John and I dropped into bed, we grappled with our feelings. We were weary to the bone, excited about the potentials and yet not sure our family was ready to handle this size of an operation. Kirsten had been a great help and worked very hard in the greenhouse, but she was a little envious of the boys' freedom to run and play. It was too much to ask that they pick berries all day, so they ended up being the local "tour guides" for visiting children. They would take them to the creek, to the hay piles to jump, or they would just sit on the porch and drink strawberry lemonade.

Usually we were very careful with our children's associations. Now we felt that we had neglected our first work. Like Jesus' parents, we had lost sight of our children for a whole day (Luke 2:43–46), and we did not feel good about that. Being solution oriented, we started thinking of how to combat this on the next picking day. Little did we know that our plans were pointless.

We must have been too busy reveling in the success to pay attention to the weather reports. This was very unlike my husband, who is typically tuned in to what's coming. That night the rain began to fall. It wasn't a gentle shower, but a torrential downpour. In fact, that remains the only time we ever woke our children up and brought them downstairs for fear of a tornado. It rained all night . . . and all day Monday . . . and all day Tuesday. The creeks swelled out of their banks.

May 6, 2003

Dear Lord, You know we're grappling with the fact that—from all outward appearances—we're losing our strawberry crop. We've had so much rain, with more predicted all week long.

May 6, 2003

Heavenly Father, the rain, without a miracle, is ruining our crop. The best crop we have ever had is about to rot in the field. Father, I must turn it all over to You. We have a greenhouse full of plants, a field full of berries, a store stocked by our hard work, spring vegetables in the field, and no customers! Yet, through it all we choose to thank You for the trials because they will strengthen our faith. Father, I embrace this trial and wait to see what You have to teach us.

May 9, 2003

Dear Lord, You know we've been struggling with our current reality—floods, rotting berries, not enough customers, etc. It appears that our future on the farm is hanging in the balance. Lord, You know that in many ways, we would like to just walk away from it all—and we will if we feel that's what You want us to do. We just need clear direction! I'm asking for some very specific prayer requests:

- Stop the rain
- Rebuke the devourer (stop the disease from spreading)
- Bring back the customers.

We don't know what to do, but our eyes are on You! (2 Chronicles 20:12)

May 9, 2003

Father, I am not an overcomer right now. It is so hard to put on a happy face and smile. We paid pickers $200 and only made $230. . . . I need to have a time of thanksgiving and praise. Thank you for . . . protecting us from the hail, . . . clearing the rain yesterday, . . . holding the rain off on Tuesday so we could get the field picked, . . . Kirsten's thoughtful and helpful ways (made lunch yesterday and wrote a note that I found under my pillow), . . . John's courage.

Even now, the memories bring back very raw feelings! After our first two days, we asked my Dad to come and help us. He gladly came and gave us as much moral support as he could. I remember John and him looking at our wet and rotting field and making the decision to rope off the bottom third and call it a loss. Much of it had been under water for days. That was a hard decision for me. I wanted to keep doing whatever it took, but the grim reality was, even if we could have picked the berries, they were so water-logged they tasted terrible. They were not even saleable! Conditions continued to deteriorate.

May 11, would have been our second Sunday to be open to the public and it actually didn't rain, but that was irrelevant. From one direction, the road to our farm was under water due to a swollen river. From the other direction, a culvert had washed out and the road was closed for two weeks. We had no good way to give alternate directions (no website back then), so who knows how many people tried to come and couldn't get through?

There were a handful of days when it didn't actually rain, but there was always a chance of rain. Very few people will travel an hour or more to pick strawberries if there is any possibility of rain. It wasn't too much of a hardship for our customers to live without our berries, but could we live without their patronage? It wasn't just the berry sales; the plants in the greenhouse were absolutely gorgeous, but it looked just as full as when the season started. Then there was the store that we had worked so hard to decorate and fill with farm gift items and goodies. The quarter acre of produce was starting to look a bit overgrown. Sitting on the porch rocking Caleb, the tears cascaded down my cheeks as the smell of fermenting berries filled the air. *Lord why? Did we miss Your lead? Why have the last five years been so hard? I never imagined it would be like this when we partnered with You.*

When I stopped asking questions and feeling sorry for myself, the thought that struck me was, *"No trial . . . no testimony."*

But Lord, what kind of testimony will we have from this? Oh how easy it is to have faith when everything goes the way we want it to, but real faith hangs on when nothing makes sense. We longed for that kind of faith and trust. We knew that the first step was to talk faith, whether we felt it or not.

May 15, 2003

Dear Lord, I've read again this morning the story of Elijah and the time of no rain (1 Kings 17). Some thoughts that I was impressed with were:

1. You led Elijah to the Brook Cherith, and then allowed it to dry up. My application: Just because You led us to farming doesn't mean that this farming venture isn't going to dry up.
2. You told Elijah exactly what to do when the brook dried up. You will lead us if we listen to Your voice.
3. You made sure that his bread and water failed not. You will provide us with what we need.
4. When we put You first, You provide for our physical necessities.

The Lord gave us the strength to face our reality one day at a time. We were learning to lean on Him and He was comforting us. Roping off the bottom third of the field was soon not enough, so we roped off the bottom two-thirds of the field. Each newly abandoned section diminished our hopes of financial success. The outlook was bleak, but we reminded each other that God had a higher reality. We must trust in Him no matter what.

May 30, 2003

Dear Lord, the strawberries are finished and once again we're back to the point of asking, "Now, what do You want us to do?" The money certainly isn't going to go very far! We don't even have the money to pay off the Visa bill! . . . We don't have money to carry on, so again we have to ask, "Do You want us to continue farming? If so, how?"

Our current reality is very sobering, but we don't want to keep trying to solve our own problems. We want to see Your hand guiding in our situation. It's clear that You allowed all the rain for a reason. We did everything we knew to do, but it wasn't enough. So, what was the reason? Do you want us to quit? I need some reassurance.

Later on the 30th

Dear Lord, when Pam revealed how bad our financial situation was, I felt I had to take some time off to seek Your will. Where do we go from here? Our situation is desperate! (We've never owed so much money and had such high monthly expenses.) We were committed to paying $5,000 to the [other] investor in our home. That leaves us $5,000, and we have to have a new car [with the addition of Caleb, we no longer fit in the little five-seater].

[The Lord led John to the story of Elisha and the indebted widow (2 Kings 4:1–7).] Principles:

- One principle which is revealed over and over in Scripture is that You multiply, use, or bless what little we have. The only time I can think of when You created something from nothing is possibly at creation.
- Another principle is that You always give the humans a vital part to play in receiving the blessings, such as the widow and sons collecting the jars.
- The blessing is only as big as the faith of the receiver.
- You give enough for the current need plus some left over, as in the story of widow's oil, and when Elisha feeds one-hundred men.
- You tell us to do with our might the work that lies nearest, and when You want us to do something different, You make that clear.

DEBT

Debt is not sin. There are those who would like to call it that, but from my study, there is no Biblical basis for this. Should it be avoided if at all possible? Yes! Is it usually avoidable? Yes! Should you determine to get out of debt ASAP? Yes!

Our society has made debt the norm, and it is often incurred for unnecessary expenditures. Getting out of debt should be a high priority—even if it means you have to eat rice and beans for a few months (or years). But, I believe there is "another side to this coin." We have seen too many people make debt reduction their god. I don't believe our Heavenly Father asks you to sacrifice your family, your marriage, or your health in order to get out of debt. Working two or three jobs to pay off debts may sound heroic, but I think it's destructive. Learning to live on less seems the better option.

The comforting reality is that God has a special place in His heart for those in the bondage of debt (yes, it is a servitude). The classic Biblical story to illustrate this (and one that has special meaning to us) is the widow and her sons in 2 Kings 4. The woman was already in debt and her creditor was ready to take her sons away. God took what the woman had in the house, asked her and her sons to put forth personal effort (and faith), encouraged her to *borrow even more,* and then performed an amazing miracle to release her from debt.

Looking back, there is no question we made mistakes when we incurred debt, but they were honest mistakes. We were seeking to follow God's will, but didn't always follow it perfectly. Some might accuse us of living recklessly, but we were certainly not living lavishly. Our testimony: God is still in the business of miraculously releasing us from the bondage of sin—and of debt!

This was a time of soul searching and reevaluating. John was grappling with God's leading and was again looking at the goals and purpose of the farm. *Why had God led us to farm?*

=== **Still on May 30th** ===

Goals for Farming:
- Be fully dependent on the Lord for our sustenance.
- Have control of our own schedule.
- Be able to work with the children.
- Be home-based.
- Have time for solitude with God.
- Provide healthy food for ourselves and others.
- Show a simpler alternative to modern life.

Statement of Purpose:
- The goal of Bountiful Blessings Farm is to provide the best conditions possible for the mental, physical, and spiritual development of our family—and yours.

Have you ever been there—knowing God has asked you to do something, but in human terms it's not succeeding? I had one person say, "I can't believe you haven't given up.... I would have quit long ago."

All I could say was, "Would you? Would you really stop doing what you were sure the Lord called you to do just because it's not meeting your human expectations?" It was perfectly clear to us both that we had been called to farm. Why it wasn't being successful, we didn't know, but we were not willing to change direction without a "thus saith the Lord." If God knew we needed these difficult experiences, we were willing to endure the trial. Yes, we did have our moments of despair, but they were usually short-lived.

=== **June 26, 2003** ===

Dear Lord, I'm discouraged! Having a hard time trusting Your leading. It seems that You haven't always supplied our needs (bills unpaid, etc.). I know that any fault through lack of faith or persevering prayers is mine, but nevertheless, I'm having difficulty believing Your Word.

I feel like we're totally lost as to how to proceed with the farm . . . the future just looks bleak! I don't even know what to ask for. Do You want us to continue? If so, I need to know how to go on. Do we look for someone to help us? Do we plant other crops? How do we come up with operating capital?

Is it time to look for other work? If so, I'd like You to make that clear to us. I would just like to hear from You, on how and where to go from here.

We clung by faith to the promise, "To all who are reaching out to feel the guiding hand of God, the moment of greatest discouragement is the time when divine help is nearest. They will look back with thankfulness upon the darkest part of their way. . . . From every temptation and every trial He will bring them forth with firmer faith" (Ellen White, *The Desire of Ages,* p. 528).

This is certainly our testimony. It was in *this* valley that God drew us near and carried us. Though we would not choose to go back there, it definitely was a high point in our spiritual journey. God brought good out of it. God *did* bring us forth with firmer faith!

CHAPTER 10

Never Give Up!

SUMMER 2003–SPRING 2004

"If at first you don't succeed, try, try again." We were willing to keep trying, but how? That was the question on John's heart as he headed for the hills early that June. The financial loss of the spring crop had caused us to question whether we were to continue farming, but God had called us to the "plow," and there was no turning back without a clear word from Him. We needed answers, we needed solutions. Determined not to take the situation into our own hands and "solve" it, John did the only thing he knew would give direction, and that was to cloister Himself with God in nature. Here we were both confident he would find answers, and solutions. Not only was John given a clear impression that we were to continue farming, and how, but God also wanted to broadcast to Middle Tennessee what was happening at Bountiful Blessings Farm.

The phone rang and the voice of the newspaper reporter got straight to the point, "Pam, I would really like to come out and do another story on your farm."

"About what?" was my cynical reply. "Really, what is there to say? We had a devastating crop in the spring and it remains to be seen if we can keep the farm open."

It was as if she didn't really hear me. She just kept on talking. "I got your letter about the 'strawberry futures' [actually we had called them "shares" but she latched on to the futures idea], and I think it will make a great story." What could I say? I told her I would talk with John and get back with her. He was no more excited about the prospect than I, but we decided we should not turn down an opportunity to speak about God's goodness and His leading in our family. A couple of days later we found ourselves once again rocking on the front porch of the barn and sharing our hearts with this dear reporter. She seemed genuinely interested and wanted to do anything she could to help. Looking back, we see clearly how God used her to give us hope and courage. Below is the article that appeared in the *Tennessean* in July 2003:

Family Not Deterred by Rainy Setback

Bountiful Blessings Farm could surely use a bucketful of blessings right about now.

The family-run farm was so battered by rain this spring that the strawberries rotted in the fields and the family did not make enough money to stay in business, according to owner John Dysinger.

But Dysinger, a former missionary, and his family of six have faith. So rather than throw in the gardening trowel, they came up with a unique plan.

They are going to sell shares of next year's strawberry harvest. Just like wheat and soybean futures – only strawberry futures.

Shareholders would have first rights to next spring's harvest, with one $25 share equaling one flat of strawberries or 15 pounds of pick-your-own berries.

"We had a lot of time to contemplate our situation as we sat on the porch salvaging half-rotten berries and looking out on the rain-soaked field,"

Dysinger said, gazing out over his berry patch.

"And what came to us was the story of Elisha and the widow," ... "He asked her what she had in her house, and the Lord used what little she had to bless and provide for her."

"Well, we're pretty well set up for growing strawberries, with the infrastructure in place," Dysinger said. "And our most valuable asset is our customers."

"So we decided to take it to the customers and tell them about our situation," he said.

"The share idea kind of evolved out of that."

His wife Pam nodded. "It's sharing the risk," she said. "For the past five years we have been taking all the risk, and this would help spread it around."

It also would spread the family's income throughout the year, with new capital providing for the purchase of soil amendments and next spring's strawberry plants. ... "Our customers have been very encouraging about it so far. They've told us they really want us to keep the farm going. But if this doesn't work, that's our sign that God wants us to move in a different direction."

While John was alone with God, the strawberry share idea formed and we sent out letters to all our customers. In this letter John explained that God had called us to serve our community by growing strawberries and if this service was to continue we would have to band together. Our customers would have to be willing to share a bit of the risk by purchasing shares in next season's crop. Because of our letter and the newspaper article, we received many messages of encouragement to press on. Those notes touched our hearts as we saw not only the kindness of customers but also of complete strangers. The article touched a resonating chord in many hearts. We felt like our arms were being held up, giving us the ability to press on. Daily, precious notes of encouragement and support came in the mail. One said, "If you don't get what you need, please contact me." One note, written by a shaky hand, described how they had been through hard times and God had sustained them. Enclosed was a check for five dollars. Day by day, as we opened our mailbox, we were strengthened to be faithful and trust in God.

One day I received a call from the precious family we had met at the Fourth of July Fair. They had never been to our farm for strawberries, but they were on our mailing list and received our letter about the berry shares. The letter touched their hearts and the wife was wondering how they could help. Not knowing what to say, and especially not wanting to lay bare our need, I simply said, "Just pray about it. The Lord will give better direction than I." Later that week, she and her children came out to pick blueberries and play in the creek. At the end of our visit, I shared a book with her that I thought she and her husband would enjoy. In turn, she handed me a card and humbly stated that the Lord had laid us on their hearts and they wanted to see the farm succeed. That evening, after we put the children to bed, we sat and looked at the card. A note of support and encouragement lifted our spirits and with it there was a check for $1,000! It seemed like a gift straight from Heaven! It was just the confirmation we needed to assure us of God's continued leading. He was showering His love on us through the generosity of strangers!

July 16, 2003

Dear Lord, I thank You and praise You for Your leading on the farm. Through the generosity of our customers, and total strangers, You have provided funds to replant the strawberries, and given us the courage to press on!

The request

"Uncle John, we would really like you to give the homily at our wedding!" This was the plea of John's oldest niece. "Do you think there is any way you could come?" We didn't know what to say. At times like this the pain of "poverty" was keenly felt. Oregon is a long way from Tennessee, and it seemed foolish to even consider the trip. Our thoughtful niece understood that finances were tight, and kindly offered to cover our gas. We assured her we would love to be there, and would pray about it. At the time, I remember wondering what there was to pray about; it seemed so obvious. But, we were learning that God's reality is far higher than our own.

Each time we took something like this to the Lord, He would remind us that we were called to serve. *But how?* we wondered. *Lord, remember we used all of our strawberry money to buy a used van? How would we cover the expenses beyond fuel?* Yes, we were going to farmers' markets, but we were not making much money. It seemed totally presumptuous to even consider a long road trip. After taking our thoughts to the Lord, we felt encouraged to make the trip. It would be a welcome change for the family, and an opportunity to experience many new places. Since we believed God was leading, we felt sure He had the solution for our finances. "Before they call, I will answer; and while they are yet speaking, I will hear" (Isaiah 65:24).

That spring John's cousin had purchased gallons of our frozen, water-logged berries. One day in early July I received a call from her. She told how their freezer had malfunctioned and they had lost all their strawberries. Amazingly, the insurance company was reimbursing them for the cost of organic berries from a local health food store. Most people would say, "Lord, thank You for these extra funds." Not this cousin! She saw it as a blessing to be passed on to us. All she asked was that we replace the berries they had lost, which we were happy to do. A few days later, a check for close to $300 arrived in the mail. God has thousands of ways to provide for us, if we will just step out and trust.

This gift was still short of what we felt we needed for our trip, but in faith we continued our preparations. I cleaned the shelves under the cash register, and my hand ran across a bank bag. It was not flat! Quickly I pulled it out and opened it up. It was full of cash and checks from one of our last strawberry days. Was it my negligence or God's provision? We believe the latter. God is so good! Our faith was growing! What if, when our niece called, we had let our current view of "reality" dictate our decision instead of taking it to the Lord? We would have missed out on a wonderful family time, and also on some amazing faith-building experiences. He guided our decision based on His reality.

Excitement built as we packed and prepared for this great adventure. We would have a *real* vacation. We visited Laura Ingalls' home place in Missouri, the Black Hills of South Dakota, and Yellowstone National Park. We backpacked in the Tetons with a four-month-old! I carried him on the front and a pack on the back! We took in our niece's romantic wedding where her "knight in shining armor" rode in on a white horse.

On the way home, we swung down through Utah to visit friends. And then we headed home. While traveling through the beautiful Colorado Rockies, our enjoyment of the scenery was interrupted by a very loud "BANG." The van started sputtering along. It sounded like we had lost a muffler. We pulled off to assess the damage, but because of the engine's location under the front seats, we couldn't tell where the noise was coming from. All we could see was that it was not the exhaust pipe or muffler.

What to do? It was almost nighttime. We were in the mountains, so there was no chance of getting into a shop until morning. The van still ran, so after a prayer for guidance and protection, we decided to limp along. I'm sure we were quite the spectacle—an old Toyota Previa van that sounded like a Harley Davidson snaking through the mountains at thirty-five miles per hour! Praise God we made it all the way to Denver! Thankfully, one of John's cousins lives in Denver. We enjoyed an unexpected visit with her while the mechanic discovered that a spark plug had shot out of the engine. Before we left on the trip, we had the vehicle tuned-up. It seems that the mechanic had not tightened down the spark plugs—the remaining ones were also loose! We were back on the road in a few hours—thanking God for His protection and mercy.

Would we trade the memories of that trip for money in the bank? Not a chance! It wasn't *our* faith alone that God was building, but also our children's faith. Staying home would have "cost" us far more.

Back on the farm

There was no time to ease into our routine. We had work to do— lots of work! The washed-out spring crops left us in need of direction on how to make it through the winter. Strawberry shares provided the means to purchase and plant next spring's crop and pay a few bills, but it would not provide for our personal needs until spring. Now we not only had a mortgage, but also a monthly payment on credit cards.

During John's spring meeting with the Lord, he had contemplated what we had "in our house." As he looked at our assets, he was impressed to utilize our greenhouse for winter production. More specifically, we wanted to start a winter CSA (Community Supported Agriculture)—where a group of individuals/families support a farmer by paying up front for the season and then receive a box of assorted produce each week. Only the Lord could have given us this idea because we certainly didn't know anything about winter production. John's farming mentor, Eliot Coleman, was pioneering winter growing in Maine. But a winter CSA was something we had never heard of. At the time, there were only a handful of summer CSAs in the Nashville area. Not having any experience with CSAs, John decided to spend a day with the most experienced of these local farmers. In many ways the visit was empowering, but when John told him our plan to have a winter CSA, the farmer was incredulous. "What are you going to grow in the winter?" John shared some of his ideas, but it really was hard to imagine how we would fill the boxes.

Our wonderful tour of the west behind us, we now had strawberries to propagate and lots of vegetables to plant for the winter CSA. We worked hard to catch up, but a glimpse into John's journal gives a picture of the challenges we faced.

========= *September 17, 2003* =========

Dear Lord, Things are looking bleak—from a human stand point. _____ [who owned a portion of our house] wants us to repay their loan right away, the strawberries are full of serious disease issues, and our winter CSA crops are being eaten up by bugs and deer. . . . Please teach us to trust in You like Caleb trusts us.

Unbelievably, after our disastrous spring crop, we were now dealing with a new batch of plants that came to us riddled with major disease issues! As always, the crisis drove John to the hills (though sometimes I drove him there). We longed for a word from the Lord. Where else could we turn? When John took time out he would often be led to different stories in the Bible. There he found principles to guide our family.

From the story of Gideon, he was impressed that God is not offended when we ask for signs. He was also reminded that God wants the glory for our deliverance. Starting with thirty-two thousand men of war, God knew they could easily gain the victory and think they had done it in their own strength. But God wanted them to learn trust in Him, so He cut the army down to three hundred, gave them the victory, and then they knew God's power had won the battle (Judges 7).

=========== *September 20, 2003* ===========

Dear Lord, we're at another crisis point—facing another long winter without enough money—plus a slim strawberry crop (or no crop at all) next spring [due to the major disease issues]. . . . I've been seeking to know Your will on how to proceed. . . . I don't want to go ahead of You. I want to wait on You . . . but I've got a family I'm responsible for! Oh God, I need divine guidance. I need a miracle. We still believe you've led us to farming but yet You allow pests and disease to ravage us. We don't know what to do, but our eyes are on You!

Three days later, on September 23, 2003, John was meditating on the story of Elijah at the time of no rain (1 Kings 17, 18). He was reminded that Elijah accepted God's promises as fact even though they did not agree with visible reality. By faith Elijah heard the abundance of rain. John was also reminded that even though Elijah *knew* God was going to send rain, he agonized in prayer until he saw the answer.

Another Old Testament story that encouraged us time and time again is the story of Jehoshaphat (2 Chronicles 17–20). Here we find steps to seeking the Lord in times of trouble:

1. Seek the Lord (don't do what you think is best).
2. Pray.
3. Fast.
4. Listen to the prophet(s).
5. Don't try and fight the battle yourself.
6. Go into the battle praising the Lord for His victory.

Those stories of great faith and trust in God inspired us with courage to press on. We were determined to trust in God's reality as we faced one financial trial after another.

TIME OUT

Calling "time out" to go to the sidelines and consult with the "coach" has been a lifeline for Pam and me on this journey of experimental religion. **Nothing else has impacted us as much!**

How does it work? Here's what we do:

1. At least once a quarter we schedule what we call a "High Sabbath" to spend with the Lord. This is a time to seek guidance for our personal spiritual walk, our marriage, our parenting, or anything else related to our spiritual journey. If we need a "business meeting" with the Lord (farm planning, etc.), we take time during the week.

2. We go out in nature. Yes, theoretically you can do this in a quiet part of the house, but there is something about being surrounded by God's handiwork that makes the time more effective. You want to limit the potential for distractions.

3. We let God set the agenda and guide our study.

4. We take our Bible and a journal. The Bible is our GPS and the journal is our record of His answers and impressions.

5. We take time to still our souls. Our minds are so full of distractions and busyness that it often takes significant time to let the Lord quiet them. We have to discipline our minds from going down rabbit trails and ask God to speak to us.

6. Music can add depth to this personal worship time. We sometimes take the guitar or flute to play our hearts out to God, but He likes a cappella singing too!

7. We make a day of it—not just a few hours. This can be a great time to fast—a time to say, "You mean more to me than food!" Sometimes we've done overnighters or weekends; whatever time you take, it's never long enough!

We've shared this "lifeline" with many people, and have been saddened to see how few actually "taste and see" for themselves (Psalms 34:8). But it has given us great joy to see our older children grabbing hold! Time out with the coach is the best way to assure you know the winning strategy. He's waiting for you on the sidelines!

~~~~~~~~~~~~~~~~~~~~~~~~~~~~~~~~~

The agreement we had with the other party who had invested in our home was a generous one. We were not asked to make any payments for the first five years. When the agreement was made, John had a full-time teaching job and we anticipated paying it off quickly. Now, eight years had passed and our investors were in need of their money. They had been so patient and understanding of our situation, and we in turn were sympathetic to their need. They generously forgave our accumulated interest and simply asked for the principle back. With no other apparent option, we headed back to the credit union to leverage our house again—making our already difficult payments almost impossible.

Planting time

Looking over the strawberry plants was depressing. It was time to plant them in the field but they looked terrible! The disease that came on the tips had strengthened its hold on the plants as they grew. We anticipated throwing away a lot of our plants. Daily we were faced with discouragement. Our debt, last spring's failure, three hundred shares (3,600 pints) of next year's crop sold (with the money already spent), the smallest crop ever, our winter crops being eaten by pests, tractor problems, and on, and on. When we focused on our feelings there was nothing but darkness.

To those on the outside, we kept up a positive, trusting front. We talked faith though we were under constant temptation to despair. Even when John and I were alone we tried to speak positively to one another. Amazingly, when one was down the other was usually encouraging. But when we were alone with the Lord, we poured out our heartache and pain. He drew us close, and through His Word, asked us to trust Him. We longed to have perfect peace and trust in our hearts but our humanity got in the way day after day. Together we bore these trials. We did not feel free to talk to anyone else. This was hard for our parents, who would have gladly helped us! But when John left teaching, we made it clear we did not want our relatives to feel any responsibility for our needs. This was *our* journey, and the Lord had called *us* to bear it in His strength alone. At times the Lord used our parents to bless us financially, but we always wanted to know it was God moving on their hearts, and not parental sympathy. This was particularly hard for my father, who wanted us to tell him our need so he could help. I remember explaining to my Dad, "The Lord knows our needs and if He wants you to be a part of providing, He will impress you to do so."

"What if I'm not listening close enough?" was my father's concern.

These were difficult times when the testing was severe. Entry after entry in my journals spoke of discouragement and despair. We left teaching because we wanted to grow closer to our children and the Lord. Were we meeting those goals? It didn't feel like it, but one thing we've learned is that feelings are never to be trusted. *One thing we did that was right was turning to God in our discouragement. He lifted us up.* He calls us to cast our cares on Him and He promises to care for us. Unfortunately, I found this hard at times and sometimes gave way to despair. On this particular day my journal revealed my disheartened state.

November 12, 2003

I'm discouraged. I find myself becoming cynical. Will things ever be different? Whatever we try to do is a flop, so why keep trying? . . . Our situation seems to bring out the worst in me. I feel like the worst wife and mother. I'm not gaining the victory over irritation. How can I when everything about my life is irritating? In fact, tonight Kirsten said to me, "Mommy, I don't know what's wrong. You've been irritated all day. It doesn't matter what I've tried to do, you just get more and more irritated." Oh, how my heart aches that my children have to have a mother like me! I just feel like the joy has been sucked out of my life. . . . I long to be an overcomer and experience deep joy.

Although there were definitely times when we gave way to the irritations and frustrations of life "on the edge," praise God this was not what we were characterized by. God was teaching us principles which were not based on our circumstances. We praise God Kirsten does not even remember this. Instead she remembers the good things we were learning from the Lord, and how we were growing as a family.

FAMILY FUN

You've heard the old adage, "The family that prays together stays together." This is definitely true, but the corollary to this principle is "The family that plays together stays together." Conscientious parents who are endeavoring to raise their children in the "nurture and admonition of the Lord" (Ephesians 6:4), often get so focused on training and correction that interaction with the children becomes very negative. We must not lose the hearts of our children while trying to save their souls. Having wholesome fun together binds hearts like nothing else.

Family fun can open the hearts of your children to the sunshine of your love so that they can more easily accept correction and discipline when it is necessary. Whether you choose to schedule it every day, or whether it's just once or twice a week, setting aside time to play as a family can quickly alter the atmosphere of the home.

What you choose to do for family fun depends largely on the age and makeup of your family, but the goals are laughter and joy. When our children were young, we played Legos and "house" together. In the summer we enjoyed freeze tag and kickball. In the winter we would move the furniture and play indoor "blind man's bluff" or "hide and seek." As our family grew up, we did more mountain biking and canoeing/kayaking in the summer and "four square" (in the shop) or board games in the winter.

Suggestions for "Family Fun":

1. Usually the best kinds of fun are simple and free.

2. It's great to share "family fun" with other families on occasion, but don't get sucked into the trap of always needing to be with others. That's not family fun.

3. Take turns picking the activity, and encourage everyone to choose to have fun—even if the activity is not their favorite.

4. Choose activities where cooperation is required; your goal is building cohesiveness, not competition.

5. Parents, this is the one time when it's okay to come down to the level of your children. It's refreshing to be like a child again!

Walls come tumbling down, negative feelings evaporate, and joy returns when you have fun together as a family. Try it! Your satisfaction is guaranteed!

John began looking for off-farm work again—not because God impressed him to, but because it seemed the only "obvious" solution. When God is silent and we press forward with our own solutions, we have found no peace. In fact, we have learned that peace is a wonderful "referee" in our hearts. When our peace is broken, we know we have stepped "out of bounds" of God's will; there is sin or self-rule in our hearts. When we confess and step back into His will, peace returns. God had other work for John to do—and lessons to teach us.

Refocusing us

Picking up the phone can change your day. Have you had that experience? The voice on the other end of the line was one from our Africa days. Yes, it was Kamwe, a young Masai boy we had sponsored through secondary school! At that time he was a Christian but had no connection with our denomination. When we left Africa, we gave him a book that later aided him in studying the Bible and joining our faith. Now he was an ordained minister, and he was in the States for meetings. He planned to stay for six weeks and wondered if he could come and see us. Of course, we said yes! What we didn't know was that Kamwe was on an ill-planned fundraising tour. He arrived at our home during the time when I was really struggling with self-pity. Now I had one more mouth to feed. Hearing about his success and what the Lord was doing in his ministry wasn't easy for me. *"Why, wasn't the Lord doing more for us?" "Does God love others more than us?" "Why do we have it so hard and others so easy?"* These were lies straight from the father of lies! The devil works the hardest when we are determined to hang on in spite of overwhelming circumstances.

Kamwe wanted to make his mission self-supporting, and God knew my husband was the one to help him with that. His idea was just to visit churches, and share the needs. How could we help?

We could hardly put gas in the car and food on the table. John took it to the Lord and was once again reminded that we were *called to serve*. What a privilege it had been to serve Kamwe as a boy. Now he was a grown man, proudly showing us pictures of his precious family. This warmed our hearts and we were humbled at the privilege we had been given to be a small part of his life. Now God was using him to reach his own people with the gospel. He shared his vision with us and what he wanted to accomplish while in the States. We were a bit overwhelmed. John started thinking and praying about a way to help, and the Lord inspired the "Sponsor a Cow" idea.

John comes from a family of seasoned proposal writers, so he began laying out a plan while Kamwe laid out our greenhouse beds. Kamwe had trained in organic agriculture in Africa so he confidently took over John's farm work.

John asked Kamwe the same question God had asked him, "What do you have in your house?" They had hundreds of acres of grazing land. The proposal God inspired would give the mission a continual source of income from the sale of cows. Sponsors could purchase a cow and the mission would sell the offspring to support their church and school. We took Kamwe to several local churches. As he shared the work God was doing with the Masai people, hearts were moved to help. The response was amazing, and money started pouring in to fund Kamwe's cow project.

Kamwe had made contact with a family in North Carolina whom he wanted to visit. They happened to be friends of ours, so we made arrangements for him to speak at their church. But how would Kamwe get there? We couldn't take him because we didn't even have enough money for gas; we looked into bus fare, but couldn't afford that either. We weren't going to ask somebody else to pay for Kamwe's travel, because we didn't ask for money. After taking it to the Lord, John felt we were to make the trip, trusting God for the details.

Over the years I have struggled with being submissive and following my husband's lead. The Lord was working with me on this. As John learned to take the lead, I learned to lay down my will and follow. If John was confident it was the Lord's will for us to take Kamwe to North Carolina, I had no problem spending the last of our money for the gas to get there. Only the Lord can give peace in such situations! John was confident that God was calling us to put our needs aside to help Kamwe, so we did.

The trip was a blessing, and money for many cows was donated. We enjoyed connecting with our friends and were reminded that "it is more blessed to give than receive" (Acts 20:35). But it is impossible to out-give the Lord. Before we left North Carolina, someone handed us a check for $500. The donor told us that the money was for our personal expenses! We were shocked! How did they know? Yes, we had shared some of our experiences, but we had talked only faith and trust. Did we say something we shouldn't have? I don't think so. I choose to believe it was our Lord! He knew our need, and as we gave of our time and resources for others, He impressed others to give to us. God doesn't stop with the basics though. He often showers His love on us extravagantly. Another dear lady came to us and asked if we had done anything "fun" with Kamwe. Puzzled, we looked at one another, wondering what she meant. She went on to say that she would like us to take him to the aquarium in Gatlinburg. We wondered how we were going to manage that! If she gave the money for him, he would have to go alone. But the lady handed us more than enough money for the whole family to go. What a treat! She had no idea that our own children had never been to any place like that! We reveled in God's lavish love as we shared this once-in-a-lifetime experience with Kamwe.

Lessons on receiving

Soon after arriving home, we put Kamwe on a plane for California where he did more fundraising before heading back to Kenya with almost $60,000 for cows! It was time for us to get back to the work of farming. We had learned some valuable lessons on giving, but God was not done with His instruction. Learning to receive is sometimes more difficult than giving. For us, this was the year God chose to give us many opportunities to practice receiving from others.

Selling Christian books door-to-door with the children provided the money to put them in music lessons. This was a sacrifice of my time, but we felt the lessons were important. Like our farming venture, the book selling did not go well. We just didn't make enough money to keep the children in lessons. The phone rang early on a cold

December morning. The voice was one I knew well. "Pam, we want to pay for Jonathan to take piano lessons next term." I didn't know what to say. For several reasons, I was not sure what the Lord's will was on this topic, so thanking her, I said I would pray about it and get back to her.

There have not been many times when I knew I had a "thus saith the Lord to Pam Dysinger" moment. This, however, was one of them. I was grappling with the question, *If God is leading us, why do others have to bail us out, and help us with our needs?* The very next morning, as part of my quiet time, I read Oswald Chambers' devotional, *My Utmost for His Highest*. The reading was entitled, "What My Obedience Costs Others." Now that was a new thought. Up to this point I had the misconception that our obedience was "costing" us and the Lord, but not others. Mr. Chambers showed from Scripture (Luke 8:1–3) how Jesus, in being obedient to His calling, was supported by others. This was a paradigm shift for me! But what an amazing thought. *We have the opportunity, privilege, and responsibility to financially help someone else in obeying God's call for their life.* That was my answer to the piano lesson dilemma. It also made it much easier two days later when we received a Christmas card from some other friends we had seen in North Carolina. Inside was a check for $585. This was not the normal way God chose to meet our needs; but for some reason, at this time, our needs were placed on the hearts of multiple individuals. That was very humbling. What if we had not been willing to go out on a limb and take that trip to North Carolina?

We gratefully accepted the kind offer to help with Jonathan's piano lessons and God miraculously kept Kirsten in lessons that term as well. Can we trust God for the big and little issues of life? Oh, yes, we can!

Serving through our pets

Service! Could God actually have a plan of service for Sugar's puppy? We had decided to breed Kirsten's dog in an attempt to raise some funds for her harp studies. The timing was perfect. The puppies would be ready for Christmas. Who could resist cute little poodle puppies with big red bows around their necks? The due date came, and we were all excited when we saw that Sugar was preparing to give birth. We hoped for two or three puppies. There was one. One large boy puppy, and he was a rather funny-looking one at that. He looked like a little Rottweiler—black with brown eyebrows and patch on his chest. We did all we could to advertise. The newspaper brought a few calls. We had no Internet back then. How life has changed! Christmas came and went and the puppy didn't sell. We were devastated. Nobody wants to spend several hundred dollars on a dog in January! When would we learn that God wants us to trust *His* timing? He can even teach that lesson through our animals. The phone rang and a lady's voice started asking questions about the puppy we had for sale. As I described his looks, she got excited. "So it's a party poodle?"

"Well," I said, "I don't know what a party poodle is but he is black and brown." The caller told me that she had looked everywhere for a bi-colored "party poodle" for her husband who had cancer. He had owned a party poodle for fifteen years and it recently died. Now her husband was facing death himself, and she had been trying for weeks to find a similar puppy. She and her daughter came that afternoon and joyfully took the puppy home. We trust that he gave that dying man some comfort during his last days.

Does Jesus care? Oh, yes, He does! He was teaching us that we could trust Him in *every* area of our lives.

Jesus cares

I awoke very early one morning in January. My mind went to my dear Nana (my father's mother). I had seen her at the time of Caleb's birth just a few months before, but for some reason I had a real yearning to spend time with her. As John woke up, I shared my heart's desire with him—knowing there was no way I could possibly make the fifteen-hour trip to her home. I prayed about it and left it in God's hands. Before our family worship that morning, John's mom called me. "Pam, I don't know why I haven't thought of this before, but I wonder if you and the children would like to go to Florida with us next week." I could hardly believe my ears! "We'll be there five days and you could spend that time with Nana and your parents." Gifts come in many packages but this was certainly an unexpected one. God is so amazing! It was on my heart, I prayed, and He gave an immediate answer. Even though we dislike being apart, John agreed that God was leading me to spend this time with family. They only had space for five so it wasn't an option for John to join us. The children and I excitedly packed our bags—anticipating a wonderful time with my Nana, as well as my parents, who lived in the other side of her duplex.

What an amazing time we had in Florida! Every day we went swimming and spent time making memories with our dear family. After putting the children to bed, I would stay up for hours talking to Nana. I helped her clean out and organize her large, walk-in closet—which she so much appreciated. While doing this, we talked about her life. Now, from an adult perspective, I entered into her joys and sorrows. It was at her knee, that as a child, I learned all those faith building stories that had given me confidence to trust the Lord for our needs. The five days went quickly, but the children and I went home with a new flush of memories to enrich our lives. Not long after our return, my Nana's health took an unexpected turn for the worse.

It was also in January of 2004, in the midst of financial trials and farm struggles, our minds started turning towards encouraging others to farm. I'm not sure how we thought we could encourage them at this point. We had embraced an agrarian life as the ideal and felt confident others could learn from our mistakes and succeed. We started thinking about seminars, apprenticeships, and having families come to the farm to learn.

January 23–25 weekend getaway

The details of this weekend are blurred with the passing of time, but the notes and content are still fresh in my memory. (In fact, in some ways I feel like I'm revealing a skeleton in our closet. That isn't easy! The only reason to reveal failings is to allow others to have the opportunity to grow from our mistakes.) Over the years we have wondered how things might have turned out differently if we had followed through on these impressions. But, we rest in the fact that God uses even our mistakes for His glory.

Whenever John and I would take time away, we would end up talking about the farm and our dreams of farm-based ministry. The Lord had impressed us that our ministry was going to be centered around the farm, and by faith we believed we would have something to share. We were so excited about the ideas God was sending our way and wrote them down so we wouldn't forget them.

The Upper Room

Purpose: To encourage families to a quieter, simpler, principled, God-directed life.

Plan: To have an upstairs apartment over a semi-detached garage. This apartment will serve as the means for a family-to-family ministry where we can share our personal pilgrimage and encourage other families to re-focus and re-direct their priorities. This apartment will be built and operated by faith—incurring no debt, and with no direct appeals for funds (unless the Lord clearly directs us to do that).

Why we feel the Lord is calling us to this:
1. We feel our family has the gift of hospitality.
2. We live in an ideal setting for this ministry.
3. Our occupation gives us the flexibility to do this.
4. We have felt a calling for some time to family ministry.
5. Our family is at a stage (age) where we can (in God's strength) model God's plan for families.
6. We feel we have the gifts of encouragement and teaching.
7. We watched the 3ABN [a worldwide Christian television ministry] story and were impressed with the way they stepped out on faith.
8. We need a focus other than the farm; we want to be more of service!
9. It fits with all our impressions about what we should be doing.

Fleece: If unexpected money is received, we will build as the money comes in.

You may think that this fleece was too easily fulfilled, but over the course of the seven years since John left teaching, we received very few unexpected donations. This one year being the exception.

Three days after we laid out the fleece, someone stood at our door, handed us a card and said a quick farewell. In the card, they shared that our family had been an encouragement and blessing to them. A one-hundred-dollar bill fluttered to the floor and we had our answer! But what could we do with a hundred dollars? We tucked it away—trusting there would be more to come.

That spring, after a weekend of company, one of our guests put a roll of bills in Kirsten's hand and told her that it was for "The Upper Room." Kirsten was to give the money to us after their departure. When we unrolled it, we found ten one-hundred-dollar bills! God was affirming His leading. We were too busy gearing up for the strawberry season to do anything with the money, so we set it aside and looked forward to starting the project some time in the future.

Was that the correct move? Should we have hired someone to do what they could with that seed money? Had we acted on this immediately, would it have changed the future? These are questions we have to leave with the Lord—trusting that even our mistakes work out for our good.

Shortly after the seed money came in, we received a call to present a gardening seminar in Virginia. Since we didn't have enough produce to keep the CSA going, we had a few weeks off, enabling us to accept this call. On the way, we visited friends in North Carolina. While there, the transmission on our van went out. The Lord was teaching us that it was not the financial loss that mattered as much as our faith and trust through the loss. We ended up staying in North Carolina for a wonderful week of fun and fellowship. That week was made even more special when many inches of snow fell. What a special treat that was for our children.

Our van took some time to fix, so our friends offered the use of their great big truck. This kindness helped us get to Virginia in time for our meetings. Riding in that fine truck was another special treat for the children, especially the boys. God had provided the money for repairs through our tax return. We certainly had other ideas about how we wanted to use the tax return money, but we believed in "first need, first claim." Seminar given and repairs completed, we headed back to the farm to resume our work. Our courage was good; we were refreshed from our getaway and looking forward to being home again.

On March 31, I received a call from my dad saying that Nana had died. Since our visit to Florida, her health had continued to decline.

March 31, 2004

She's resting! My precious Nana just simply stopped breathing. . . . [She's] resting until the trumpet sounds and she is called forth from her dusty grave to meet her Lord. Oh Father, it makes my heart yearn for You. . . . You are so loving and so faithful. . . . You were so merciful to me in giving me those five days with her in January. I never dreamed they would be my last. I cherish the memories of staying up late and talking. She told me many stories about her life. . . . [She had] so much wisdom to share. . . . [She was] so thoughtful . . . so kind . . . so caring. She will be greatly missed by many, especially me!

Now we faced another question. Should we make the trip to New Jersey for her funeral? Considering our financial stresses, the answer seemed obvious, but we were not accustomed to making decisions based on financial reality. John prayed about it and felt we should all go; family was more important than finances. Did the trip add to the financial stress? Yes, it probably did, but I am so glad we went! People are more important than bank accounts. The little we might have saved by staying home was much less significant than the memories we made. This was the first time since my childhood that my Dad and his sisters' families had all been together. We visited the places that were near and dear to all of our hearts, and reminisced about the blessing Nana had been in our lives.

Gentle reminders

When we left teaching, our goals were to draw close as a family and cultivate a deeper relationship with the Lord. At times we lost sight of these goals, but God was so merciful that He gently reminded us and called us back. We were learning to listen and each obedient response made the next one easier.

===== *April 20, 2004* =====

Dear Lord, I thank and praise You for the way You're speaking to me. Lord, I'm a slow learner, but if You're patient, I think we can do this! The other day You impressed me to close up the canola oil pesticide container, and I disregarded the impression. Within a few minutes, the container had spilled on the ground! Then yesterday morning You impressed me on my walk to go back and pick up that dying worm on the road. When I obeyed, You gave me a beautiful illustration of what You've done to rescue me. Then You also prompted my thoughts on agriculture. The reason agriculture is so hard is because Satan is trying to discourage people from going into it. It's Your original plan for man and so Satan is going to do all he can to foil that plan. You placed man in a garden, Satan is trying to take man out.

Lord, I continue to pray about our financial situation. We need money now to pay late bills. But, we're trusting in You for deliverance—attempting to seek first Your Kingdom.

The financial struggle continued, but through it we experienced peace. I longed to receive the kind of faith that would trust God even when the cupboards were empty. In his mercy, He never allowed it to go that far, but it was close. On a challenging day in April, the Lord again spoke to me through Oswald Chambers. In a devotional called *The Dilemma of Obedience*, he writes, "Every time circumstances press, say 'speak Lord.'" That was all we wanted! We were confident of God's leading, even though, outward circumstances offered plenty of reason to question that leading. John and I were always united in our belief that God had led us to this. Therefore He must know that we, two rough stones in His tumbler, needed these experiences.

Taught by a dog

One day we were all outside working. Our faithful sentinel, Sugar, sat in her usual place on the back of the couch, looking out the window—longing for us to come home. Sugar does not eat or drink when her loved ones are out of her sight. I came back to the house and when she caught sight of me, she started to bark. This was normal. But as I got closer and called to her, Sugar barked all the louder. This was not normal! The ultimate insult came when I reached out to pick her up and she turned on her heels and ran away from me as if I were a total stranger. Just then the thought came to my mind, *That's just what you're doing to Me.* Ouch! *Father, forgive me for my short-sighted view and lack of trust in your character. Give me more faith and trust.*

It was strawberry time again but the crop was doing poorly. This was expected because the plants we purchased the previous fall were of such poor quality that we composted more than a third of them. We planted the other two thirds with little assurance they would survive. In the fall, my father made a fourteen-hour round-trip to purchase more plants from another farmer. These plants were beautiful and made up for the third we had to compost. By spring the one-third of the berry patch that was home to the new batch of plants promised a good yield.

Rain. . . . *Lord, not again,* we pleaded. Memories of the previous spring were still like an open wound. Did we trust God? Knowing that two thirds of the field had intense disease pressure made us all the more concerned about the rain which created the perfect condition for the spread of disease. Fortunately, the rain was sporadic and we were able to keep the field picked clean. For strawberries this is very important. After three weeks of picking, the diseased part of the field was totally wasted. We were left with the plants my father got, and praise God they did well.

The three hundred flats ($7,500) of berry shares that had been paid for in the fall came off the top of our earnings. We met all our shares and made a little money beyond that. Was it enough to sustain us through the summer? No. We were headed for another rough year, but until God released us from farming, we knew that, at all costs, we must press on. He had been so faithful to us during this growing season. Our first winter CSA did fairly well. The "berry shares" would again provide the capital to replant next spring's crop. Decisions had been taken to the Lord and He had given us answers as well as solutions. He was faithful, and we were determined to be the same. We didn't feel like there had been very much succeeding, but we were willing to try, try again.

CHAPTER 11

Letting Go

SUMMER 2004–SPRING 2005

"Be sober-minded; be watchful. Your adversary the devil prowls around like a roaring lion, seeking someone to devour" (1 Peter 5:8). Have you ever felt him hunting you down? We have! The following is an excerpt from John's "Surrender" sermon:

> It was a Friday. Our adversary prowls hard on Fridays. There was much to do on the farm. Couldn't get mowers out because the tractor was in the way. Couldn't start the tractor. Remembering that Dad said there was a problem with a battery cable that got fried. He did say that he could start it with jumper cables, so I got those out and hooked on to the battery—which wasn't easy. Tried to start. Nothing. Fiddled with cable connections—still nothing. Decided to replace ground cable. Trekked down to the house, got cable, and discovered a missing bolt. Walked back to the barn. Hooked cable on—none of this was easy. I'm convinced that someone has a job of making things as awkward and inaccessible as possible. Got the cable on, but

still missing the bolt to clamp cable to terminal, so I scrounge around and find one that turns out to be a hair short. Did our best to get it to work, but it wouldn't fit! Scrounged around some more and finally found a bolt the perfect size—even fit nut we had. Praise the Lord!

Tried to start. Nothing. Checked around some more and discovered that the main wire from the battery to the starter is fried. Tried to take off engine cover, but one bolt was stuck and I couldn't get it to budge!

The Lord has given peace up to this point, but I'm about to lose it. All I wanted to do was mow! So I decided it was time to flee the temptation. Tractor will have to wait. We had to come up with a different way to get the mowers out. Moved stuff and made a pathway to the other door of the barn. After all that one mower wouldn't start and the other one had a flat tire!

Do you ever have days like that? Well, at times we felt as if our whole life was like that! Surrender has a twin sister and her name is Trust. Where there is complete trust, it is not difficult to surrender. This is a key God was trying to teach us!

Surrender again

Lying in the hospital bed hemorrhaging, I had to surrender the life of our unborn child. In the spring, just before the strawberry season, I had made the alarming discovery that I was pregnant. This was our one and only surprise pregnancy, and I'm ashamed to say I was not delighted. Yes, we wanted another child so Caleb would not grow up alone, but in my mind it was too soon. It took some time to come to peace with God about this, but the peace and joy did come and the children's enthusiasm and joy were contagious. As I neared the end of my first trimester we begin telling others our good news. The cool responses were painful. That was hard, but God was giving us real joy over this new life.

Children are a blessing from Him, and we were certainly loving the larger-than-average family God had given us. As I lay in the bed, I cried out to God for peace. Why had the baby died? I wanted desperately to trust Him completely. Finally, I surrendered all of my plans and my will. Peace flooded over me and I was at rest.

It's one thing for us to gain the victory, but how could we expect the children to understand and trust? They were devastated when we shared the final outcome. They wrapped their arms around me and hot tears of disappointment rolled down their faces. They had already taken this little brother or sister into their hearts. "Why did the baby die?" they wondered. Drying their tears, we called them to trust Jesus. We shared how He had given us peace and trust. Then we pointed them to trust.

Children are so resilient—especially when parents talk faith and trust. Little did we know that just six months later we would again pass through this "valley of the shadow of death" (Psalm 23). With that final miscarriage my dream of having a sibling close to Caleb's age died. I accepted the fact that Caleb would have a very different life than our other children who grew up together. Again we comforted our children and ourselves with the words of Scripture; there we found hope. It is not for us to ask why. It is for us to accept God's providences. Miscarriages are riddled with guilt, questions, and blame. What could I have done to prevent this? It's harder yet if you know there are things you should have done. Again we cried out to our Heavenly Father and He gave peace. We dried our tears, talked faith, and praised the Lord for the children He gave us.

Summer

Our summer was busy with a large garden as well as some storage crops like potatoes and squash for the winter CSA. Continuing the strawberry shares in July brought in money to purchase the tips and prepare for propagation. By the middle of August we were busily mixing soil, making blocks, and planting those sixteen thousand runner tips. The numbers we planted each year varied some as we tried to find the ideal plant density per acre. Healthy looking plants gave us reason to rejoice. There was no sign of the disease that had plagued the previous year's crop.

We began to prepare for our second winter CSA. The first year we had twelve families. We hoped to increase that number considerably. This was to be a main source of income and we believed God would provide what we needed.

The only challenge was that our faith and our visible reality were not congruent. We were learning to trust but it wasn't changing our financial situation. I should not have been surprised. I prayed that God would keep us in this difficult situation until we learned the lessons He knew we needed. We were in cooperation with God; we trusted that whatever we were going through *was* for our best good—and also the best thing for our children.

We did not burden the children with our discouragement and struggles. We took our complaints directly to the Lord. To the children, we talked faith. I praise God for helping us to win this victory! Our children knew we were having tough times but they never heard us blaming or distrusting God, so they didn't blame Him either. They saw me taking more walks. They saw John regularly heading to the hills for prayer. But we were determined not to talk about our wavering faith or the burdens that overwhelmed us. I didn't talk about the lack of food. They did not hear me complain about the shortage of funds. Why did we keep it from them? We wanted the trials to strengthen their faith. The only way that would happen was to let them hear us talking faith and trust. By God's power we did this.

Now, back to our reality.

The financial stress of two consecutive crop "failures," as well as doubling our mortgage, made the struggle increasingly intense. It was a hand-to-mouth existence and at times we felt the hand wasn't even reaching the mouth.

August 20, 2004

Oh, Lord, why has the path been so hard? . . . Why do our crops fail? Why do bugs devour? Why does frost kill? . . . When we say, "God has called us," I imagine others saying, "Boy, I hope He doesn't call us."

These were real struggles, but we chose to believe that ultimately everything we were experiencing was for our best good. We hoped that all of this would somehow benefit others as well. God's ways are so far above man's ways! We have grown up in an independent, self-improvement society. It is assumed that if you think positive, improve all your opportunities, and work hard, there is no need to trust God. We might give lip service to trusting God, but do we really? What if we woke up one day and all our earthly supports were gone? The bank account, savings and investments gone, no insurance of any kind, simple food in the pantry. Would we trust then? We must! There is no question that God had the power to make the farm successful; we were certainly doing our part. But we were in the Lord's classroom. He knew what lessons we needed and when.

〰〰〰〰〰〰〰〰〰〰〰 *August 24, 2004* 〰〰〰〰〰〰〰〰〰〰〰

Yesterday as I studied and prayed I felt You were saying that we should simplify our lives by selling our house and building in the barn.

This was not a thought out of mid-air. As John and I brainstormed about how to proceed, it seemed the only possibility. That little log cabin by the creek was my dream home. I was intimately involved in its planning and construction so you would think that the idea of selling it would be very painful to me. Praise the Lord for a "peace that passeth all understanding" (Philippians 4:7). I am a sentimental person so it was a miracle that I could surrender my home so willingly. Change is difficult for me; but the desire to follow the Lord surpassed my desire to stay in my lovely little log home by the creek.

Determined to find out if this was the Lord's solution for our financial problems, John headed to the hills. I worked in the greenhouse and the children played nearby. I stood at the bench, seeding soil blocks. The thought crossed my mind that I should go to the barn and prepare my heart and mind to make it my home. I dropped what I was doing and walked up to the barn. I stood there and looked at it, trying to imagine how we could make this cold, drab place into a warm and cozy home. It seemed impossible. But I knew that if God was in it, He would help us to accomplish it.

When John arrived he found me at the greenhouse. The first words out of his mouth were, "Honey, let's go look at the barn." I wish I could say that there was a twinkle in my eye and a smile on my face as I said, "I've already been there." In reality, it was still a little difficult. Quietly I admitted to my husband that the Lord had already prepared me to accept His leading in turning the barn into our home. Gathering the children, we went to the barn. There John shared the impressions and study of his day. Moving to the barn seemed to be the only way to stay on the farm. Our children could not imagine leaving the farm and certainly didn't want their Daddy to take a "real" job away from home, so they intellectually accepted the fact that this was what needed to happen.

Once the decision was made, it still took the children some time to adjust. Looking back, I wish I had been more sensitive to their pain. The Lord had so freed me from sentimental attachment that I wasn't as sympathetic as I should have been to what the children were going through. This was their home and they loved it! All their childhood memories centered around that home and the creeks and hills surrounding it. Jonathan was particularly vocal about not wanting to move to the barn, and rightfully so. If you had seen the barn at that point you would be able to understand his concerns. Joshua was young enough and easygoing enough to just accept life as it came. Kirsten struggled with many mixed emotions. She was old enough to understand our dilemma and desired to support our decision. Still, it was a huge loss to her—one she felt keenly for a number of years. The setting of the cabin was lovely! She loved her little room that looked out over the family garden. She and the boys had spent hundreds of hours playing in the creeks that ran in front and to the side of the house. When we left the cabin, she left her childhood with it. The bottom line: change is hard!

It was hard for those who loved us to think of us living in the barn. One family member, upon hearing of our plans, wanted to see what we were thinking. Taking her up to the old barn, we shared our vision for the place. With heartfelt concern she stated, "You can't live here! This place is unfit for human habitation." But when God calls, He gives a vision and a plan. He didn't ask Noah to come up with plans for the ark. A tabernacle in the wilderness seemed totally impossible, but God gave Moses the plan, talents and abilities, and made provision for the materials. Did God write out a plan for us? No, but He inspired us with ideas and the ability to imagine the end result.

John's parents were so supportive through it all! It was difficult for them to watch us struggle year after year. Respecting our need for privacy, they never asked probing questions. By this time though, we could not hide the fact we would lose the house if we didn't do something quickly. There was no way we could continue farming with our current mortgage. They understood that. Even from their perspective there was nothing to do but sell. Our major concern with selling the cabin was, who would buy it? Its location made it an integral part of the farm. When we built there, we had the unstated agreement that we wouldn't sell. Separating it from the rest of the farm was difficult. We would have a neighbor. That was a sobering thought. Though peace reigned in my heart, I began praying for five specific things:

1. Someone who will feel good about paying the price we need.
2. Someone who is older or single—no children.
3. Someone who loves the log home look.
4. Someone who would receive a blessing by being near our farm and family.
5. Someone who would be ready to move fast!

In September, our next strawberry crop was set out and prayed over. With high hopes we did all we knew to do and trusted God to give us a good harvest the next spring.

The Winter CSA would start October 15. We had twenty-five families that were planning to participate. This would not be enough to live on and run the farm as well. We had hoped for more CSA members, but God knew we had only enough produce for that number of families. We accepted what came to us with thanksgiving.

Needing some spiritual rejuvenation, we headed to northern Georgia for a weekend camp meeting. There, we reconnected with an old friend from college days. It was wonderful to catch up on one another's lives. Before we left on Sunday, our old friend handed me a vocal CD that she had recorded. I gave her a quick thank-you and we parted ways. During the next few weeks, as we grappled with the sale of our home, the Lord ministered directly to me through a song on that CD. It was Isaiah 41:10, 13, 17:

> *Fear not; for I am with thee: be not dismayed; for I am thy God:*
> *I will strengthen thee; yea, I will help thee;*
> *yea, I will uphold thee with the right hand of my righteousness.*

> *For I the Lord thy God will hold thy right hand, saying unto thee,*
> *Fear not: I will help thee.*

> *When the poor and needy seek water, and there is none, and their*
> *tongue faileth for thirst, I the Lord will hear them,*
> *I the God of Israel will not forsake them.*

What comforting words! I took that CD with me when I traveled in the car. It was the only place we had a CD player. I just listened to it over and over and over again. As the tears streamed down my face, I asked God to give me the faith to believe those promises.

We did not want to give a realtor the meager profits we might gain from the sale of our house, so we decided to try selling it ourselves. We put a sign out by the road and began to spread the word that it was for sale. This brought us several interested parties, but no one was ready to act. We prayed earnestly for the Lord's will, trusting He had the whole situation in His hands. One serious interest arose. For several weeks the potential buyers went back and forth as to whether it was the house for them. Finally they came to the realization that it was not the house for their family and the Lord led them in a way more suited to their needs. We were happy for them, but that didn't solve our problem. John and I continued seeking God's guidance. We prayed for wisdom and moved ahead—trusting that He would shut the doors if we were out of His will.

October 22, 2004

Father, please, rescue the perishing. You are keeping me at peace, but my enemy is constantly attacking me with anxious thoughts and feelings. Oh Father, please help us.... I can only think that you want our testimony to be "peace amid the storm.".... I thank You for what You will do. I know that You long to be glorified.... Keep me resting in You today.

November 8, 2004

Dear Lord, I just need your Holy Spirit in my life and family! I want to be single-minded for You. Lord, You know we're in a financial bind again (we seem to stay there most of the time). We need to sell our house, but we don't have the money to fix it up or advertise it. You know our other needs. I don't believe we are being lavish or extravagant with our money. We are just talking about the basics. Lord, I'm asking for at least $500 from one of Your thousand ways to provide for us. And please either bring a buyer for our house or else show us another way out. We're trapped at the Red Sea [see Exodus 14] and need Your deliverance.

We both spent many hours sitting by the creeks or walking to the pond. When alone in nature, I would cry out to the Lord, asking Him for peace. He promises that if we seek Him with our whole hearts, we will find Him (Jeremiah 29:13, 14). God kept affirming me through His Word, through nature, and through song that He was in control, and that His ways and plans were far above ours. True to His word, as we focused on Him, our hearts were filled with peace.

On November 17, I was working around the kitchen when I had a wonderful thought, *God doesn't just want to meet our basic needs. He wants to exceed our expectations. He has something special in store for us.* That thought gave me a lot of joy! I didn't know for sure if this was my own thought or if it was the Lord's. I just tucked it in the back of my mind for future reference. If it was just wishful thinking, time would tell.

A few minutes later, there was a knock on the door. To my surprise, in walked Mike. He didn't live locally, but would occasionally show up to work on the house he was building just down the road from us. Loving to give, he would often bring a little surprise for our family. He handed me a box, hugged Sigmund and Sigfreid (his nicknames for Jonathan and Joshua) and off he went. In the box I saw several jars of peanut butter and a few cans of soy milk powder. What a blessing! Those were staple items we didn't have in the house. Of course Mike didn't know that! Then, as I glanced back into the box I noticed something that he had never given us before—and something he never gave us again. It was a jug of pure maple syrup! Pulling it out I scanned the label—questioning whether it was really what it said. I opened the lid to smell it. Sure enough, it *was* maple syrup! This was an amazing treat for my family! Limiting ourselves to one pancake with maple syrup per breakfast, we nursed that jug along for months. With each serving God reminded us He wanted to pour out an extra special blessing for our family. To my heart, the message was loud and clear. God was not simply going to give us the basics—like peanut butter and milk powder. We were to expect the syrup! What a boost to our courage! It gave us confidence to trust that God really *was* going to untangle this mess we were in.

Looking back, I stand in awe of how beautifully our Heavenly Father worked out all of the details of our situation. The tapestry of life is intricately woven on the loom of Heaven! Can I unravel it simply enough for you to follow? I will try.

We have a long-time friend named Wendy who lives on the west coast. Over the years, we pretty much lost contact with her. She was aware of the fact that we had left teaching and begun farming. That fall, Wendy contacted us about purchasing a box of organic produce as a gift for a woman who lived about an hour from us. This woman was the author of a book which had been a real blessing to Wendy. In an effort to thank this author, Wendy wanted to give her some produce from our farm. Arrangements were made and we eventually found ourselves sitting in our living room visiting with the author. One of the beauties of farming is the fact that it connects you with many people who otherwise would never cross your path. After an enjoyable visit, our new author friend gathered the vegetables, and with many words of appreciation, went on her way.

That afternoon I called Wendy to give her a report of our visit with the author. She was glad to know how much the lady appreciated the produce, and that we had a nice visit. I shared some other experiences with Wendy. Full of enthusiasm, she encouraged me to write a book. I shrugged it off. John was too busy, and I am not a writer. Moving on in the conversation, I shared our current need to sell our home and asked her to pray for us. I told her that we wanted God to bring just the right buyer. It was quiet on the other end as Wendy listened. She asked some questions about the house which I answered without much enthusiasm. I did not want to jump to any conclusions about a potential interest on her part. Wendy just kept on asking questions, and I kept on answering them. Then she asked if we could send some pictures.

Wasting no time, we put some pictures and a short video together and got the package in the mail to Wendy.

November 22, 2004

If all our transactions cleared we would be $177 in the hole. We are putting our trust in You, asking You to rescue us somehow from our difficult situation. Father, please relieve us of the financial burden of our house. We need to be rescued! We really do feel like life has . . . Just forget where this comment is going! I have hope and peace in Your plan. . . . I trust that You can keep me from anxious thoughts today.

November 24, 2004

I sent the pictures of our house and farm to Wendy yesterday. We just ask that You would go before them. You guide! Our one goal is that You would be glorified in our lives. . . . Thank You for peace. Our hope is in You!

Praise the Lord; He was teaching me how to control my expressions even in my journal. Everything I was feeling did not need to be expressed. I was learning to talk faith.

Edwin, Jennifer, Caroline, and Paul (John's oldest brother and family) planned to spend their Thanksgiving vacation with us on the farm. We wanted to stay together. Mom and Dad were away, so they were happy for us to use their spacious home. We packed to move up the hill for a few days—having no idea we would never spend another night in our little cabin.

November 27, 2004

Yesterday John told me that he won't have enough lettuce to provide for our customers so we may have to shut the CSA down for a few weeks. We can't pay our bills as it is. What do we do? My faith looks up to Thee. I know that the more bleak our situation looks, the more glorious Your solution will be. You are not going to hang us out to dry. I praise You and thank you for trusting us with these trials. Of course my humanity hopes that at some point we can move on from this recurring theme, but only You know if or when that would be safe. For today, I'm thankful for peace.

On Thanksgiving Day, I was reminded that twenty years ago I had been with Wendy at her parents' home. Making a quick call to wish them a happy Thanksgiving gave me the opportunity to see if she had received the pictures. Wendy answered the phone in her usual bubbly way, and we talked for a few minutes. She then confirmed that she had received the pictures and was very interested in our home! I did my best not to let any hopes or expectations slip out, but inside I was jumping for joy.

One thought troubled us when we considered selling our house. God had confirmed that we would be doing family ministries through "The Upper Room." How did the sale of our home fit into that plan? We had started a non-profit foundation called *Blessings Shared*. This was in preparation for the ministry the Lord was calling us to. Nothing was really happening with that, but it was in place and ready to go when God opened the doors. An idea began forming in our minds. Maybe someone would purchase the cabin and donate it to *Blessings Shared*.

That would fulfill the Upper Room concept while getting us out of debt. The only problem was that we could not talk to anybody about this idea. We felt committed not to solicit funds unless God specifically impressed us to do so, and He hadn't given that direction.

November 30, 2004

Yesterday we had a wonderful season of prayer. We told the church family we are asking You to secure our house for ministry purposes. We continue to ask that You will make our house available to Blessings Shared.

Looking back, I can't imagine how we thought we could convince *anyone* to start farming based on our experience. But, we serve a merciful Father and I believe He kept that vision before us to give us courage and strength to continue. The thought that our trials were not simply for our blessing, but would help and bless others, spurred us on.

Studying the Scriptures changes our concept of time and of God's will and plans. Moses knew he was to deliver God's people, but it took forty years for him to get ready for the job. Abraham was told he would have a child by Sarah, but they waited twenty-five years. At the age of twelve, Jesus knew He was the Messiah, the Lamb of God, but it was eighteen years before He began His active ministry. God often reveals a plan that takes years to unfold. We see clearly now that neither we nor our farm were ready for a more public ministry, but God, in His mercy, showed us that our experiences would someday help others. He would allow us to work with Him in leading people back to the garden.

November 30, 2004

Dear Heavenly Father,

I am weary of financial strain. I want a little money to buy Kirsten something for her birthday. I want to get some small thing for the boys . . . but as usual we have nothing right now. This time of year is always hard. We get Christmas cards and we can't even send one—no money for stamps. Oh well, it makes life simpler. Father, I don't want to be discouraged or unwilling to go on. Please, help me. Guide me today in the way I should go and show me how to live a life of peace and joy. "Do not forsake me, O Lord; O my God, be not far from me! Make haste to help me, O Lord, my salvation!" (Psalm 38:21, 22).

Eight o'clock that evening Wendy called.

December 1, 2004

Loving and Merciful Father,

Yesterday I wanted to call Wendy but John said we should just wait on You so I just prayed. After we put the children to bed I sat looking at past journals for encouragement. My reflection was interrupted by the phone. She is serious! . . . This really seems like the "syrup" You impressed me was coming!

December 5, 2004

Dear Lord, You have truly showed yourself strong on our behalf this last week! It appears that Wendy is going to buy our house! The way it has all worked out definitely makes it seem providential. The thought of getting out of debt is so liberating! Lord, we've learned our lesson. Keep us strong to "owe no man anything."

We had "moved" up to Mom and Dad's for Thanksgiving and just stayed. I'm not sure why. Looking back, I wonder why we didn't go home for one more Christmas in the cabin. In many ways the break was less emotional since there was no time to think, "This is the last time . . ." I know that would have been hard for all of us.

We believed the sale of the cabin was to enable us to get out of debt and keep farming. At the same time, we didn't want to jump to conclusions. Did God have other plans? Was our farming experience over? We prayed the Lord would make it very clear to us if He planned for us to make a move. Just a year before we had been approached about a pastoral position. Now was the time for a change if a change was God's plan. A part of our hearts longed for a change; anything other than farming! We looked into one job opportunity that seemed interesting. A caretaker was needed for a retreat center in the eastern mountains of Tennessee. After visiting the location we felt sure that this was not

God's will. We were burned out on farming, yet, deep in our hearts we knew God had not released us from this calling.

We made plans to start building in the barn. John's dear parents suggested that we move in with them on a permanent basis. Their house did have ample room for us all. But we had a family of six. It just didn't seem that invading their space would be the best thing for our long-term relationship with them. I have always been terribly independent and the Lord has dealt very firmly with me on this point. Our reticence to move in with John's parents was something different from personal independence. John and I were in agreement that it would be hard on both households to live long-term in the same house. The hustle and bustle of childhood and youth is challenge enough for parents to endure. Grandparents deserve peace and quiet when they want it. They were generous to offer, and we were grateful for their willingness. At the same time, we felt the Lord was leading us to build in the barn. It would be a long, drawn-out project because we agreed to build only as time and money were available.

January 1, 2005

The sun is setting on this, the very first day of the new year. My life is so full of blessing. I have a husband who loves me and lifts me up. I have four beautiful children. We are so fortunate to live in this serene and peaceful place. . . . I am blessed far more than I deserve!

You have walked with us through every difficult time. You rescued us through the sale of our house—lifting the burden of debt. I have full confidence that no matter what comes in '05, You will be there for me. I'm learning to lean. . . . I'm learning to trust.

January 15 was the closing day on our house and the paperwork was finished. Wendy was not planning to move to our area right away so she wanted us to finish the house and get it ready to rent. The next couple of months were spent working on the cabin—hiring and overseeing workers to finish the trim work and paint. It went well. We slowly moved all of our belongings up to the barn.

The reduced financial stress was a huge blessing, but other trials continued to test and shape our characters. Trials seem to come in three categories: financial, relational, and physical. For eight years we had struggled financially. When this type of trial diminished, the others increased. We now faced some challenging issues at church. There were differing views on spiritual truths and applications. It was very difficult for us to share our concerns with the pastor. We were outside of our peace-loving, conflict-avoiding comfort zone. God allowed these trials to stretch us in different ways, and to prove our willingness to stand for principle. We did not feel a bit good about being labeled as "Pharisees."

We wrestled with God's Word and asked Him to show us if this label was fitting. Were we being legalistic or simply following truth? I clung to the promise, "Thou wilt keep him in perfect peace, whose mind is stayed on Thee: because he trusteth in Thee" (Isaiah 26:3). When my peace was broken, I knew I was not focusing on Christ.

Five years earlier we had felt the call to leave our comfortable church family, which was all our children knew. We began to help a dying little church with just a few older members. John preached twice a month while the children and I helped with music and did anything else we could do to be a blessing. Once a month we went back to our home church where our membership remained. The rest of the time we were "missionaries" to the little church. Separation and service were just what our family needed at that time. Now we saw that the differences in viewpoint were doctrinal, and not easily reconcilable. We felt God was setting us free to return to our home church. The children rejoiced. Every Sabbath we would be worshipping at the church they had always loved. There we had dear friends, grandparents, aunts, uncles, and cousins. It was a wonderful reunion.

To everything there is a season

April 6, 2005, 6:30 a.m.

I'm sitting in our empty cabin, the home where so much of life has taken place. This house holds so many memories I couldn't begin to recall them all. . . .

In a nearby town there is an Amish woman probably experiencing similar feelings. Moving out of a house they built. Away from a community they grew up in.

Change . . . it's part of life in this world. Father, help me to embrace it, to find joy
in new beginnings. We're thankful for the freedom that change can bring. . . .
Thank You, Father for making this change as easy for us as possible.

Our Amish friends were going through their own hard times. This family was excommunicated from their church due to their convictions that Saturday was still the Sabbath. They were shunned by family, and their land was sold right out from under them. They were people without land, house, or supportive family. Wendy heard of their plight and was touched by their sacrifice for the sake of their convictions. She worked out an agreement with them and they were moving into the cabin the next day.

Spring, our busiest season, was fast approaching. Frost protection had started—which meant interrupted nights, but that was not much of a hardship in the face of a good crop. After successfully protecting the crop, the next hurdle is the weather during the harvest. This year it was perfect! Every Sunday, Tuesday, and Thursday was dry—enabling us to keep the field picked clean. We struggled some with disease, but since overwhelming rains did not come, the disease was kept in check. Every flat of berries we picked we sold—as well as meeting all of our strawberry share responsibilities. Unfortunately, our yield was still well below average. In those years, we did not have enough money for the soil amendments that increase production. It is a vicious cycle: if you don't have money to amend the field in the fall, production is diminished in the spring, which makes it hard to afford the amendments in the fall, and so on.

That year we made enough money to replant the crop and squeak through the summer, as long as we were very frugal. The winter CSA helped some in the fall. But we still fell far short of making enough money to run the farm and also provide the bare essentials for our family. So what were we to do about building a home? I struggled with the realization that we were not able to start building that summer. Once I accepted this, I had tremendous peace. We looked forward to a slightly easier schedule and a lot less stress.

In June, John had his annual Farm Business Meeting with the Lord. They hashed out the future of the farm. John's question, as usual, was "Where do we go from here?" What followed were ideas and LOTS of numbers and speculations—farmers are great at that. During this meeting with the Lord, John first acknowledged his wish for someone to work with him part-time. The burdens of farming were great. John was tired. We had invested everything we owned in gaining knowledge and laying the foundation.

In response to those thoughts, we pursued a couple of possibilities for help, but the Lord just closed the doors. Instead, He confirmed that we were to press on with the farming alone, trusting Him for strength.

We did not know that help was on the way! But first there would be "mountains" to climb and "valleys" to pass through.

DECLARATION OF DEPENDENCE

We are taught from an early age that the goal of "manhood" is to become independent. A boy moves from one end of the spectrum, total dependence at birth, to the other end, being "on my own," at age eighteen or twenty-one. This independence is encouraged, admired, and celebrated by our culture.

There *is* an independence from the world's systems that is admirable (i.e. energy and food independence), but I question society's whole emphasis on "independence." Is it Biblical? Jesus said, "I can of mine own self do nothing" (John 5:30). He also says to His disciples, "Without me ye can do nothing" (John 15:5). The problem with the Laodicean church is that they feel they have need of nothing (Revelation 3:17). They think they are independent, but God tells them that they are actually in a wretched condition and need to feel their total dependence.

I would like to propose a paradigm shift away from celebrating our independence. From my personal experience and study, I suggest that the spectrum should go from total dependence on our earthly parents to total dependence on God. Why else would Jesus encourage the rich young ruler to sell all that he had (Luke 18:22)? Why else would He commend the widow for giving her last two mites (Mark 12:43, 44)?

He wants us to feel keenly our dependence on Him, "for when I am weak, then am I strong" (2 Corinthians 12:10). Now that is something to celebrate!

CHAPTER 12

Changes

SUMMER 2005–SPRING 2006

Have you ever wondered why God does things in twos? Like Moses and Aaron, Caleb and Joshua, John the Baptist and Jesus, and then sending the disciples out two by two. There is a time to be alone. Moses was forty years in solitude before he was called to work with Aaron; then God called them to labor together to deliver God's people from bondage. Only God knows when solitude is to end, and partnering is to begin. God had a plan to expand the influence and ministry of Bountiful Blessings Farm, but He knew we could not accomplish it alone. Our faith and family had grown tremendously and we were encouraged by the direction in which the farm was going. Yet we were weary from the physical, emotional, mental, and financial strain. We had spent eight long years in the school of hard knocks. We longed for graduation. We believed God had special plans for the farm, but it didn't seem that we could ever achieve them alone. Knowing *how* to make the farm financially successful, and being able to actually *do* it were two separate things. We had laid the foundation of a wonderful ministry/business, but had invested *all* of our earthly resources and energy in that foundation. There was nothing left to "build the house." While God was preparing to send us help, we were off chasing the rabbit of part-time employment. That was no problem for God; He knows how to direct and redirect those who are seeking to do His will.

The summer months on a farm are always busy! The grass, vegetables, and weeds all grow like . . . well, like weeds! They demand constant care. We were no longer going to farmers' markets. Our only income was the strawberries and the winter CSA. This was not easy, but it worked out better than anything we had done before. The farm was finally paying us a small salary every month!

In July we had an extended family reunion. The most memorable part was a survival trip that my boys and their male cousins planned. Our rough-and-tumble Dysinger girls still have some hard feelings about being excluded. The activities we planned for them just didn't quite match up to the boys' grand adventure. Of course the dads went along too. Special concessions were made for Grandpa who was seventy-eight at the time. He got to bring some extra bedding. Everyone else was limited to a fanny pack holding a survival "blanket," matches, a small amount of trail mix, and some salt to season the wild things they would find to eat. There were also a couple of machetes.

Our boys and John, Grandpa, three uncles, and four cousins made up the group. The three-day adventure started off with a trip to an all-you-can-eat restaurant. There they consumed enough food to last for days. Once in the woods they discovered there was absolutely nothing they could find to eat. Can you imagine going on a trip with a group of growing boys with only seasoned water to "eat"? Then the rain began. The trip coincided with the remnants of a tropical storm. Tree branch shelters don't do much to keep the occupants dry. A memorable time was had by all, but cousins Stephen and Nick prevailed upon the group to shorten the last day and return to the all-you-can-eat restaurant. Today that trip makes for wonderful story-telling!

Family time has always been very important to us. During those years when money was in short supply, we never missed a reunion on either side of the family. It was *always* a financial sacrifice and it often left us eating many meals of rice and beans to catch up, but missing those events would have made our children feel deprived. Do we regret making family gatherings a priority? No way! The memories of those wonderful family times are still sweet.

We propagated strawberries in August, and prepared for the winter CSA. Day by day, our courage grew. We remained confident of the Lord's leading. Looking down toward the cabin, I saw those sweet Amish children playing in the yard, and my heart was warmed. Look what God did! He provided for their needs and ours at the same time. Peace reigned in my heart as I marveled at God's miraculous provision through the sale of our house. We were not yet building our barn home, but I was content.

Rabbit chase?

In September we were first exposed to the "Sharper Minds" program which helped children with learning challenges. It was a multi-sensory approach that combined physical and mental exercises. The program achieved great success with a wide range of children. Because things were always so tight on the farm, we wondered if John should supplement our income using his background in education. The Sharper Minds program seemed like the perfect solution. We hoped that it would also help us with some of our own home-schooling challenges. We prayed about it.

Once again we set out sixteen-thousand strawberry plants and prayed for God's blessing. We still used the woven plastic to cover our raised beds. This reduced our weeding to pathways and a four-inch hole around each plant. At last the strawberries were actually a money making proposition! In addition to our delicious spring strawberries, we were quickly gaining a reputation for our super sweet winter carrots.

Growing carrots, like all the other tasks on the farm, taught us many life lessons. Agriculture is God's classroom, and those who listen will hear Him teaching important lessons that affect every area of life.

A weed-free patch of plants is really quite simple in theory; get the weeds when they are young. The old saying, "A stitch in time saves nine," is so true! But, we were often too busy to do that one stitch in time. In that case we had to do the nine instead. Rather than being on our feet for a few days, hoeing around the carrots, we found ourselves on our hands and knees for weeks, pulling by hand the weeds that threatened to choke out our crop and rob it of vital nutrition. Oh how often we spend our lives trying to weed out negative traits of character which could have been cultivated out easily when we were young!

Along with farming, we continued to investigate the Sharper Minds business. John had all the qualifications to license the program. The Lord seemed to be opening the doors. John and I, along with one of our children, planned to fly out to Oregon for an evaluation and training process. We decided to take our three older children through the program in order to gain experience and learn whether the process was beneficial for them. Their experience would indicate whether we should offer it to others.

The night before we left, I got a call from another farmer's wife in our area. We have known this family casually for years, but it was very unusual to get a call from her. During our conversation, I told her how the Lord seemed to be leading us to this educational program. In return, she shared with me some challenges they had gone through with one of their children. She said that they were helped by some vision therapy similar to what I was talking about. Her words of encouragement were so affirming! We gained additional confidence that God must be leading. On October 11, we boarded a plane for Oregon and there began a program that would have a large effect on our family.

As soon as we arrived home, we began the program with our children and started seeing almost immediate results. For example, Jonathan, who was twelve at the time, was reading at his grade level, but getting him to sit still long enough to read was nearly impossible. I had to require him to read for fifteen minutes a day. This was a real trial for him. Less than a week after we started the program, I "caught" Jonathan reading a book! I could hardly believe my eyes. This had never happened before. For him, reading was never for pleasure. Quickly I exited the room. Looking at the clock, I took note of the time. Forty-five minutes later, Jonathan emerged. I'm sure he was shocked as I hugged him, saying, "Do you know what you just did?" Bewildered, he said, "No, what?" Thus began, what we believed to be another avenue of ministry which would nicely complement farming.

A different sort of Thanksgiving

Thanksgiving 2005

Heavenly Father,

Your mercies are new every morning and I am the honored recipient.

This year we are having a different kind of Thanksgiving. It's a pleasant difference. We spent the morning helping friends work on their home and then had a big group over for lunch. . . . I pray that You will continue to give contentment and peace as we await the timing to build in the barn. . . . You are our only need and I pray that our children will see that having You in their hearts is their greatest need. Empty me of self and fill me with Your Spirit today.

I will be the first to admit that it is easier to "rest and trust" in the Lord when everything is going just fine. For us, those times were a welcome oasis; they never seemed to last long, but they surely gave us strength to face the next challenge.

It was the first part of December when our van broke down. We towed it to a mechanic and awaited the word.

Resting, that is what I'm doing. I can't do anything about our housing situation and I can't do anything about our car, so I just rest. Father, thank You for giving me the ability to rest in You. Even when the details of life seem stressful, You can and do bring peace.

That resting continued even when we got the word that the head gasket on our van was blown. The age of the van and the awkward location of the engine meant that it was not worth fixing. Now we had to come up with money for another vehicle. I didn't know what we would do, but somehow I remained at peace. My in-laws gladly shared their van with us for a few weeks until we were able to get another one.

December 17, the day before Kirsten's fourteenth birthday we got the shocking news that her cousin Stephen, may have lymphoma. They were still testing and would know more soon. The next day, on her birthday, we received the devastating news that it was more likely an incurable form of cancer. Dazed by this, we found it difficult to do any celebrating. Two days later the diagnosis was confirmed: Rhabdomyosarcoma. This is a very aggressive form of cancer that primarily attacks boys at the onset of puberty. Stephen was about the same age as Kirsten and Jonathan! Again, it was a call to trust. We must trust that our Heavenly Father, who loved Stephen far more than even his parents could, had weighed and measured this trial. Daily we lifted them up in prayer, talked faith, and prayed for God to be glorified in Stephen's life.

A new chapter begins to unfold

Soon after the beginning of the new year, Edwin (John's brother) and his family started talking to us about moving their family to the farm. Edwin had, for several years, felt the Lord calling him to some form of agriculture. While visiting in Tennessee we had once said to him, "If you feel called to farm, why don't you join us?" The Lord was not ready back then to terminate our time of solitude, and His plans for Edwin's family would keep them from joining us for two more years. But now the decision was made; they would be moving to the farm in June.

The plan was for Edwin's family to live upstairs in Mom and Dad's house; Mom and Dad would remodel the apartment we were in, and we would finish our barn home. The only problem was that we didn't want to go into debt and we didn't have any money. Now what? It is easy to look back and wonder, *What if . . . ? Did we think seriously enough about living with Mom and Dad?* but all I can do is relay the facts.

A couple of months prior, John did an in-depth study on debt. He had come to believe that it wasn't a sin to be in debt, but that it should be avoided wherever possible. Now we could see no way to avoid it. We had to move out of Mom and Dad's apartment in June. So on January 26, 2006, we once again tied a noose of debt around our necks.

February 13, we began building in the barn, and what a beginning it was. What the devil meant for our harm, God used for His glory. Years earlier, when we built the store in the barn, we put a storage loft above it. Now our house plans called for relocating the stairs. This was the first task.

John stood on the edge of the loft, working from the top while our Amish neighbor and his boys worked from below. It is a pole barn with posts twelve feet apart. John was placing a new 2" × 10" × 12' between these posts. This beam would anchor the staircase. But John forgot one critical thing. The middle twelve-foot section, where he was working, was actually 12' 6" wide. Leaning over, he placed one end of his 2" × 10" × 12' beam on top of the stud wall below. When he went to set down the other end, he realized his mistake. John was off balance, and falling head first toward the concrete floor below. With all the strength that a burst of adrenaline can give a terrified man, John's feet pushed off the sub floor. Leaping horizontally, he caught hold of the top of the stud wall in the room below. There he swung, his feet dangling two feet off the floor. Those watching stood with mouths gaping open—amazed at what had just taken place. They said it was like slow motion as John gracefully pushed off, flew through the air, and gently came to rest hanging from the wall below. Shaking, John let go of the wall, and dropped gently to the floor. There was no hard landing. There were no bruises. There was no soreness. There was only God's mercy!

One of the "plusses" of life

God cares about the big and little details of our lives. Even when we can't see how something could possibly work out, He is behind the scenes, laying out a plan. Kirsten had wanted to play the harp. Ever since she was about five years old she would make play harps with clothes hangers and rubber bands, but she really wanted to play a real harp. We didn't see how that could ever happen. Have you ever met a farmer's daughter who plays the harp? We did pray about it, and we left it with the Lord. If the harp was a part of God's plan for Kirsten's life, then He would make it happen.

When Kirsten was ten, we had an opportunity to start her in group lessons on a 14-string harp. A year and a half later we pooled our resources and purchased a 38-string lever harp. Her long-term goal was to have a 46-string pedal harp, but in the meantime, she was quite content with her lever harp. We all realized that if she ever got a pedal harp, it would be years in the future. During this time, Kirsten was teaching the little girl who had bought her original 14-string harp. This girl wanted to move up to a lever harp, so Kirsten kept an eye on the websites where used harps are advertised. One day, while we were working together in the greenhouse, Kirsten mentioned that she had seen a used pedal harp listed for half the normal price. She didn't say or think anything more about it.

The next morning, I felt impressed to look for that pedal harp on the Internet. I communicated with the owner, and arranged to talk with her on the phone. She was just finishing high school and heading off to college. She hoped to be a missionary nurse, and she didn't see the harp fitting in with her plans. As we talked, I felt sure that this harp was for Kirsten. But, how would we pay for it? It seemed impossible. The first hurdle would be selling Kirsten's lever harp. I called around to some of Kirsten's harp friends who were now teaching. One of them had a student who was actively looking for a lever harp. The friend thought that her student might be very interested in Kirsten's harp. If we sold the lever harp, we would have almost half of what we needed for the half-price pedal harp. Kirsten had saved up some money. If we could make up the difference, she could get her heart's desire. After praying about it, John and I both felt we were to go forward in faith.

Without Kirsten's knowledge, I sent pictures of the harp to Kirsten's teacher who owned the same model. We arranged to have Kirsten play this pedal harp for her next lesson. She usually played the teacher's lever harp so Kirsten came out of her lesson with a big smile on her face. She told us how her teacher had let her play one of the pedal harps. I asked her how she had enjoyed it. The excitement on her face verified the words she used to tell us that she loved it! With that assurance, I called the young lady in Ohio and told her we would like to come and look at the harp. Behind Kirsten's back, the family was bursting with plans to reveal the big secret to her. And what a wonderful surprise it was! Kirsten was shocked. She could hardly believe this was happening. Together, she and I made the memorable six-hour trip to secure the harp. It was difficult to spend even the "little" that we did on this harp. I wrestled with God about how expensive harps are, but then the thought crossed my mind, *there is no amount of money too extravagant for God's honor and glory*. So we committed Kirsten's harp ministry to the Lord and asked Him to use it and bless it. He has done that. Kirsten's harp has allowed her to play in many settings where we would not otherwise have had opportunity to minister. More than this, heavenly music has filled our own home. God is good!

Winter CSA and on to spring

The winter CSA was becoming the heart of our farm. It provided us with a small but steady income. It was good to have something that we could count on. Once we secured the customers, we didn't need to worry about marketing. We could just focus on growing quality produce. The CSA was far more relational than the strawberries because we saw our customers every other week for six months. We saw most of our strawberry customers only once during the spring rush. We were building relationships and serving. This is what God called us to. As we learned more about winter production, we were confident the CSA would continue to grow. We were now delivering to large surrounding cities. There we found an anxious, wide-open market. In the dead of winter, delivering fresh produce harvested that day was like delivering a dose of mental and physical health. It was not just food. It was like a gift. Opening their boxes, our customers would exclaim in amazement at the beauty, variety, and freshness of the produce. This was something they could not get anywhere else. It was extremely gratifying!

Even though the winter production was going well, we still depended heavily on the strawberries to get us through to fall. While we lived on top of the hill with John's parents, monitoring our crops and protecting them from frost became much more challenging. The temperature is sometimes ten degrees warmer at their house than it is down where the fields are. We were learning how to manage the crop from a distance, but were still prone to making disastrous errors. All went well through March and the first part of April. Just when the field was full of blooms and setting fruit, we again faced the harsh reality that in some parts of farming there is no margin for error.

April 8, 2006

Father, how could we be so distracted? How could You let us both blissfully sleep with not a thought of our berry crop? I think we are numb to the berry woes; tired of the challenges. One mistake, like last night, and you lose it all—or was Your protecting hand over it? Father, please for Your name's sake, honor, and glory, spare our crop and we will give You all the praise. If not, we will press on as You direct. Thank You for the peace that I know You can give even if we have been hit hard. . . .

I read all my underlined verses from Psalms 1 thru 37, and my heart is strong. The Lord **is** our refuge, strength, shield, guide, and protector. The promises of help are sure. No matter what the outcome of today, I will trust Him. Our Father knows what we need and how best to lead us. My trust is in Him and I have no fear.

Later: We were hit hard! I'm sure it could have been worse. It was a costly mistake! Father, we ask for You to bless and multiply what is left.

What God did after this strawberry disaster we can't know for sure, but what we can say is, He knows how to give peace to His people in spite of disastrous circumstances. By the first of May, we were in full production and again interacting with our customers as they brought big, beautiful strawberries out of the field. Every year they said the same thing. "These are the best strawberries I have ever tasted!" or "I think they're better than last year!" We gave praise to God for multiplying the berries and making them beautiful, big, and sweet. Interacting with customers in the field, or sitting in the rocking chairs on the porch was very gratifying. This year we met all our share obligations and made a good profit beyond that. Our hearts were full of gratitude. This was our livelihood, our ministry, our calling, and people were paying us to do it! In the warmth of a beautiful spring day, the trials of winter melted away, and we couldn't help but praise God for His faithfulness through it all.

Progress on our barn home wasn't going very fast. Building in a barn is easier in one way and much more difficult in another. The "rustic look" does not require the same degree of carpentry skill, but because nothing is square, every cut is custom. John now juggled building, the farm, and his educational business, which was doing well.

Edwin's family was soon to arrive so we prepared to move into the store area of the barn. It was like a game of "fruit basket upset." Edwin and Jen would live with Mom and Dad. We would vacate the apartment so it could be renovated. Our house wasn't finished yet, so we would live in the lower part of the barn. I am so thankful that God's grace is always there to supply my need! It was not easy to live in such confined quarters. There were no windows—just rough openings which gave easy access to the cats who took pleasure in pouncing on us in the middle of the night. There was no shower, no stove, no refrigerator, no washer or dryer. All of these were sold with our cabin. We had only a sink, a toilet, and a two burner hotplate. In spite of the inconveniences, we were at peace. We knew that most of the world's population live in more difficult conditions than this. Every time I was tempted to feel sorry for myself, the Lord would bring the poor of this world to my mind. Our "poverty" would seem like great riches to so many. We did our best to make it a fun adventure for the children. Every morning and evening we gathered on the porch for our family worship. We sang to the birds and they sang to us. It was a blessed bonding time as we shared one room and roughed it together.

～～～～ LOWERING THE STANDARD OF LIVING ～～～～

Okay, I know this is a little radical, but I would like to challenge you to lower your standard of living. Here are a few of the reasons why:

1. Living in Kenya for six years showed us in graphic color the abyss between the rich and poor. One thing that

amazed us was how the poor always had their doors open and wanted you to come in for tea. The rich lived in self-made prisons—with bars on the windows, barb-wire-topped-walls around their houses, and armed guards. The poor seemed to be the happier ones.* We want to keep our doors open!

2. Ronald Sider's book, *Rich Christians in an Age of Hunger*, had a profound influence on our lives. The bottom line: How can you live an affluent lifestyle and call yourself a Christian while much of the world doesn't even have the basics (food, water, and shelter)? It doesn't mesh! Besides this, there are not enough natural or man-made resources to allow the world to live like we do. We can't just try to raise their standard of living, we've got to lower ours. It is a moral imperative.

3. Accumulating "stuff" does not bring happiness and fulfillment. In fact, the opposite is true! Stuff clogs our lives, ties us down, steals our time and energy, and wearies the mind. Freeing our lives of clutter gives us time and energy to focus on relationships which are really what matters in life.

4. You will have a hard time trying to get rich at market gardening! The lifestyle is not conducive to affluence. The only way it works is by slimming, simplifying, and living on less.

Are you convinced yet? How about this: "Take heed, and beware of covetousness: for a man's life consisteth not in the abundance of the things which he possesseth" (Luke 12:15).

*I'm not talking here about those in abject poverty. We saw plenty of that too. But even they often seemed happier than the rich!

Our third winter CSA was behind us, the spring crops were finished, Brighter Futures (our educational business) was going well, our solitude was coming to an end, and a partnership was about to begin. Life was good and we relished the changes. We looked forward with excitement to what God had in store for Bountiful Blessings Farm.

CHAPTER 13

Our "Brighter Future"

SUMMER 2006–SPRING 2007

"Hindsight is 20/20," they say. Sometimes that is true but in our experience it isn't always the case. Sometimes hindsight is 20/20 only when viewed through the eyes of faith. At every step of our experience we were truly seeking to follow the Lord. Does that mean the direction was always clear? Does that mean we did everything correctly, or that we followed His leading perfectly? No! There were "whys?" sometimes. But God promises to make even our mistakes work out for our ultimate good. Every experience in life, both good and bad, has the potential to strengthen our faith, shape our character, and teach us deeper trust.

Our nephew Stephen was rapidly declining in health. We longed to see him before he died. Everyone in the extended family had made the trek to California and spent time with him. Everyone, that is, but us. We talked about making a trip, but didn't know how or when. After a particularly strong week for Stephen, we talked with his parents, Wayne and June. They were excited about plans for a camping trip the following weekend. Could we come? This, we thought, was the perfect time! John's *Brighter Futures* business was doing well. He could counsel his clients by phone for a couple of weeks, so we decided to go.

Sunday, July 15, we piled into our van and began the three-day trip to Southern California. Two days into the trip we got word that Stephen had taken a turn for the worse. He was slipping in and out of consciousness. We all felt the temptation to question, but as John and I trusted, it was easy for the children to follow our lead. We drove long hours for almost three days in order to arrive early on Tuesday afternoon.

Wayne, June, and Stephen were in the bedroom. We waited patiently for them to call us in. The sight that met our eyes was a shock. Our once strong, handsome, lively nephew was hardly recognizable. He looked so frail and weak in what seemed like such a big bed. Love filled our hearts as he turned to us and said quietly, "Thank you for coming." Those words of appreciation made the thirty-six hours of driving all worthwhile! He knew we were there and he knew who we were. We praised the Lord that we made the trip when we did. We told Stephen that we loved him. His quiet "I love you too," was sweet music to our ears.

Kirsten had made a digital slide show of Stephen's life. The pictures and music made a deeply moving narrative. When she showed it to him he said, "It's just not fair that I'm so tired." We didn't want to tire Stephen any more that day, so we soon went off to the home of our kind hostess.

The next day (July 19), John and the boys went to see Stephen again. This time he was much more alert. Kirsten and I, busy helping with various things, visited with him briefly in the evening, I remember thinking how much better he seemed.

July 20, 2006

6:00 a.m. Good morning, Father. I'm here to gain strength for this day.

6:30 a.m. Dad came over to tell us that Stephen is dying. . . . "Blessed and holy is he who has part in the first resurrection. Over such the second death has no power" (Revelation 20:6).

It was around one o'clock in the afternoon when Stephen, cradled in the arms of his parents, went to sleep. It was a sleep like that of Lazarus; only Jesus can call him from it. Stephen's fight for life was finished. His life was an inspiration to many. Because he looked forward to Jesus' return, Stephen was not afraid to die. Even in death, God was glorified through this young man's vibrant and trusting outlook on life!

We wanted to stay for the funeral services in order to give whatever support and help we could to the family. We also didn't want to be in the way during the days between Stephen's death and the funeral. We decided to take the children camping in the mountains. We were disappointed that we could not do this with Stephen, but we chose to talk and think faith. God's plans and ways are so far-sighted, and ours are so short-sighted; we could trust our Heavenly Father who loved Stephen so much more than we.

John grew up in this area so he chose one of his favorite childhood camping places. We were blessed with a few quiet days to grieve, to process our feelings, and to talk with the children about their feelings. This was the second time our children had to face the death of a beloved peer. Praise God for the simple, trusting faith of children.

We were so blessed to learn that Stephen, shortly before his death, had ministered courage and comfort to his pastor. The pastor had said, "Stephen, this must be so hard for you . . ."

The response was, "Why? I'm just going to go to sleep, and the next thing I know, I'll see Jesus coming!"

Every event surrounding Stephen's death was seasoned with the intimacy and deep love of his parents. They knew how to set the mood and bring beauty to life's hardest spots. The funeral service reflected all of the love they had for their son, combined with their faith in God. We went to California hoping to be a blessing to Stephen and his family. We left there knowing that we had received the greater blessing.

On our way home we spent a couple of memorable days mountain biking in Utah with my brother Greg and his family. They had moved to Colorado three years earlier. Our boys had long dreamed of biking in Moab, so we seized this short moment. The strenuous physical exercise was good medicine for aching hearts. Time flew by, and long before we were ready for goodbyes it was time to go home.

Back on the farm, life was getting more intense. There was just too much to do! It was the first part of August. John was preparing to have a booth for our *Brighter Futures* at a nation-wide teacher's convention being held near our home. All of the teachers in our denomination's vast educational system were coming together for a few days of inspirational meetings and training. Tom Hunt, our good friend from Africa days, was attending the session. He decided to come a few days early and spend some time with us. God knew we needed counsel from someone who understood our journey, who loved and cared for us, and who was standing on the outside looking in.

Two days into his visit, Tom sat us down and got straight to the point, "You all are trying to do too much." We were "camping" in the bottom portion of the barn. We were attempting to start a business, we were building a house, and expanding the farm to satisfy the needs of two families. We were so busy looking at all the things that needed to be done that we were not able to see the bigger picture. With Tom's help, we brain-stormed about our options. He encouraged us to take a break from the farm for a season. "Try to get the barn livable and the educational business on a more stable footing," was his advice.

We took Tom's counsel to the Lord who confirmed the wisdom. Praise God for true friends who leave you better than they find you! We talked with Edwin and Jennifer and together decided that they, with the help of our children, would grow the strawberry crop for the following spring. We did not offer the winter CSA. What a relief!

In November, just two years after she bought our home, Wendy felt God leading her to sell it. Her purchase of the house had been a huge blessing from God to us, and also to the Amish family who had lived there. We praise God for Wendy and her generous spirit. Now we faced familiar fears; who would buy "our" cabin?

But God called us to trust, and we did. What a relief it was when Edwin and Jennifer felt led to purchase the cabin. The Lord worked out all the details. Edwin worked hard to keep the sweet Amish family there, but they saw God leading them in another direction. We couldn't understand their reasoning at the time, but looking back it's perfectly clear. God did amazing things in their lives through trial and triumph in the following years. None of us knew then that God was making that house available for someone in Edwin's own family. God orchestrates our lives for blessing to every individual as well as the whole. We *can* trust Him!

The *Brighter Futures* business was just that for us. This was *our brighter future*. With no real effort or advertising, John had ten to twelve clients in the program. We cherished high hopes that, with a little work, the business could grow to be a comfortable part-time job. Because we lived so simply, it could meet our financial needs and John would then get back to farming the other half of the time. Then there would not be such a terrible financial burden if crops failed to do well. This plan sounded very good to me. I loved farming, but I was weary of the financial stress. I had always prayed that the Lord would not release us until we had learned the lessons He knew we needed to learn.

Had we learned all of God's lessons? Apparently not.

John was determined to do everything he could to start the business right. He set up an office in a spare room at his parents' house, and then we advertised. We passed out brochures and visited private and public schools. We picked up one more client in September, none in October, and none in November.

Moving into the barn house

On the third of November we decided that the upstairs of the barn was ready for us to move in. It was by no means "finished," but we thought that it was livable. There was no functioning kitchen. There was no heat. We thought that it would surely be a bit warmer upstairs than downstairs. The first ten days were very cold days. John scrounged to find the parts he needed in order to renovate our wood-burning stove which had been sitting idle for the past two winters. We lived in coats, hats, and boots, and were sorely tempted to feel sorry for ourselves. But we chose not to yield to those temptations. I reminded myself and the children that when Laura Ingalls was a little girl, they often woke up with snow on their beds. At least we never experienced that!

Living in "difficult" circumstances is character building, and something to be embraced. As a society, we are "soft"—too accustomed to a life of ease and plenty. I recognized that these challenging experiences were exactly what we needed. They made us stronger and taught our children to be adaptable. When we finally found ourselves standing around the wood stove soaking up the warmth, we appreciated the simple comfort more than we had ever done in our lives before! At last we had heat! There was one small challenge though. You had to stand right beside the stove to feel the warmth. That is rather inefficient as far as productivity goes! The first floor had no windows, doors, or insulation, and there was no insulation between downstairs and upstairs. It was impossible to keep the house at any decent temperature. The bundling continued. We often ate our meals huddled around the stove. Whenever any sympathetic soul expressed the concern that we were deprived and suffering, I would reply that we had never found snow on our beds. The hardy founders of our nation were men and women who could endure difficulties. We aimed to count our blessings while learning to be a little tougher ourselves!

No Brighter Futures clients came on board in December or January. The financial panacea was not panning out, and the stress increased.

A turning point

In the middle of January, John and Edwin left the farm to attend an agriculture conference. I stayed home with the children. After lunch one day Kirsten made her regular trek to the mailbox and back. Glancing through the mail, I saw an all-too-familiar envelope from our bank. I knew what it held. Slipping into my bedroom, I opened the white envelope and confirmed my fears: our bank account was overdrawn. I hurried out of the house and headed to the old barn on the other side of the creek. I did not want the children to see the tears streaming down my face. I felt that their faith was my responsibility, and I didn't want my momentary discouragement to have a long-term effect on them. Opening the creaky, old door, I climbed into the hay and bawled like a baby. I longed to trust the Lord for everything, but how could I? Hadn't He let us down again and again? It was a harsh and devastating realization that after all these years, after all the Lord had done for us, after all my desire and effort to have faith, I still did not trust Him. I berated myself for failing to trust; I struggled with the Lord for failing to take better care of us. I felt He was not being trustworthy. Years of pain and frustration that I thought I had surrendered came tumbling out. Wallowing in these thoughts and feelings brought one flood of tears after another. How could I be so unfaithful? If God were just more faithful! What kind of Father would lead His children into a "wilderness" where they would have all human support cut off, and then fail to meet their basic needs?

When the tears finally dried up, I started to ask the Lord about our situation. We were $333 in the hole, with no savings and nothing in our business account. He impressed me that, when we are following Him, we *always* have what we *need* for that day. I argued that I didn't have what I needed. The impression was clear that I did. I had the habit of stashing a little money now and then for some specific need. The Lord reminded me of my stash. I argued that it was for something else, but He reminded me of George Müller's approach, which had become ours as well, "First need, first claim." I was also reminded of a small, hand vacuum that John had just purchased; I could take that back. John had change in his drawer. I had a few dollars in my purse. Peace began to return, and with it came remorse for failing to trust the Lord. He had always been so faithful and I so unfaithful, yet He still loved me! What an awesome God we serve! He loves sinners! Like Peter, I had denied my Lord. Like Peter, I had also seen the error of my ways and forgiveness was extended to me even before I asked. What a merciful Savior! "For as the heavens are high above the earth, So great is His mercy toward those who fear Him; As far as the east is from the west, So far has He removed our transgressions from us. As a father pities his children, So the Lord pities those who fear Him. For He knows our frame; He remembers that we are dust" (Psalm 103:11–14).

Kneeling in the hay, I asked the Lord to embed this experience in my heart, never to be forgotten. He had provided and would continue to provide for our daily needs. Today that meant enough money to get my bank account out of the hole. Peace returned to my heart as I crawled out of the hay and headed home to see for myself how God was going to work.

I pulled out my little stash, gathered all the change in John's drawer, and collected stray bits of money that were left here and there. Next, I counted all of the cash and added the amount to the receipt for the vacuum that I planned to return. It was enough! Of course it was! God had said in His word that He would provide our "daily bread." Trials often came along on Fridays when we needed to get ready for the Sabbath. This time was a case in point. With high spirits, I charged the children to do their best to clean and prepare for Sabbath while I made a necessary trip to town. They didn't ask any questions. Why should they when I was visibly happy and radiating peace? I drove straight to the store to return the vacuum, then to the bank, and then back home.

As the Sabbath approached, I felt like a different person: I *was* a different person! I am now more confident than ever that my Heavenly Father will always provide for my daily needs. If it isn't provided as I think it should be, then I trust He knows my needs better than I. We have had many financial trials since this time, but I can say it has never been the same. Somehow this experience brought me to a place where the Lord could break through and change my heart. Praise God! I still have moments when there is a crisis of trust, but when those times come, the Lord reminds me of my time of wrestling in the old barn and trust is more quickly re-kindled.

When John returned home, I shared my experience, and we rejoiced together. The work of building trust is not something that we can accomplish for one another. We can encourage each other, but we must individually learn to trust in the Lord in every situation. John had his own moments of doubt.

─────────── *January 24, 2007* ───────────

Dear Lord, I realize that I am still struggling with real issues of faith. Yes, I believe . . . yet I don't really believe You will supply our material needs. I truly want to, and am endeavoring to seek first Your kingdom . . . [but] our material needs are not being met. . . . Sometimes I think I need to just go out and get a "real job." . . . My heart's desire is to be "God-employed." . . . Lord, I just wish You could make it crystal clear to me what my part is in providing for my family and what Your part is. I'm willing to do whatever You lead me to.

No clients in February. No clients in March. Our financial situation was desperate! The Lord had done a great work in my heart, but my human nature easily forgets God's promise to never leave or forsake us. Though He had revealed Himself to me just a few weeks earlier, I was daily involved in a real struggle, as for life itself. The Bible does not teach once saved, always saved. Likewise, there is no guarantee of "once trusting, always trusting." It's a moment by moment choice to surrender and trust. I continued to grow, and to choose trust, but life was difficult and the devil was right there to tempt me to disbelief.

〰〰〰〰〰〰〰〰〰〰〰 *March 12, 2007* 〰〰〰〰〰〰〰〰〰〰〰〰〰〰

Father, thank You for what You are doing in my life. Thank You for the trials. . . . How "secure" I feel with money in the bank and how "insecure" I feel when there is nothing and we are totally dependent on You. Intellectually I know all the right answers, but my peace is not unbroken. Thank You for loving me enough to keep working with me, to keep me in a place of total dependence and total peace. . . . I just pray that You will keep me faithful as times get tougher. . . . Show me moment by moment how to roll my burdens onto Your shoulders. . . . Thank You for this "wilderness" experience and for the "promised land."

Extravagance, foolishness, irresponsibility, or faith?

Our children (ages 15, 13, 11 and 3) felt the need for more fellowship and association with like-minded companions, so we planned a trip to visit some friends in a nearby state. The time for the trip approached, and we felt keenly the fact that we didn't really have the money to go. Twice in the past we had scheduled a visit and cancelled. This time when John took it to the Lord he was impressed that we should plan to go—even though we didn't have money for gas. That was faith stretching!

The day before we planned to travel, John received a *Brighter Futures* check in the mail. It came from a delinquent client that we had written off as bad debt. The check was just enough to make the trip! Isn't God amazing? What if we hadn't taken it to the Lord? Logically it was foolish, but God sees what is around the bend, and asks us to move forward in faith. Again our faith was strengthened. After the fact, we shared the blessing with our children. They saw that we were willing to do "crazy" things to meet their need for fellowship, and they also saw that God was interested in their longing to spend time with friends. It didn't end there. Our loving Father went "above and beyond," to show us that investing in our children is never a waste. The day of our return we received another unexpected *Brighter Futures* check which covered some bills that had accumulated on my desk.

Experiences like this taught us that God wants us to lay ALL of our plans before Him—even those that seem so obvious that we don't want to bother Him about them. We have done *many* things that didn't make financial sense. Some seemed downright irresponsible. But whenever we took our decisions to the Lord and followed His lead, He has filled our lives with rich experiences. Our God does know how to give His children good gifts, but often we are too fearful to trust.

GIVE THEM THE BEST

As we searched and studied God's counsel on parenting, we learned about the replacement principle (illustrated in Luke 11:24–26). When you "clean the house" of the things God tells you to eliminate, you don't want to leave the house swept and empty. You need to replace the negative with positive things or the negatives will come back stronger than ever. As a friend of ours says, "Give them [your children] the best, and guard them from all the rest."

We didn't want television, high-speed Internet, video games, or motorcycles, to name a few of the world's distractions. So we attempted to replace these things with family reading time during long winter evenings, family work times like cutting wood together, and family fun times in the great out-of-doors. We gave our children free time to ride mountain bikes, to roam the woods and fields, and to build forts, tree houses, and vine swings. No, we didn't do it perfectly, but I think we can honestly say that our children's lives were so full of the best, that they didn't have time to fret about what they were missing.

Too often we see conscientious families seeking to keep their children from the evils of the world without providing better alternatives. What are urban or suburban children supposed to do with their "free time"? Unfortunately, these children often spend their time and energy pining for the "leeks and melons" of Egypt (see Numbers 11:5). One beauty of farm life is that there is no time for pining. Plus, if our children want leeks and melons, they can grow them!

Now we started to wonder what the Lord was trying to tell us about the educational business. In addition to our local clients, there were a number of clients in Chattanooga, three hours away. John had to drive to the city every other week to work. He spent time in marketing. He needed time in the office each day to get better acquainted with the program and add his own personal touch. He studied to stay on the cutting edge of brain research. Despite all of these efforts, the business was not growing. Finally, it fizzled out completely. We were confused. Finances were *very* tight. We had not received any salary from the farm for eight months and it would be another five before we started our next winter CSA.

To compound our confusion, John's brain research studies confirmed what we had always believed: nature, or "green time," played a vital role in the development of a healthy mind. Hard work, requiring both mental and physical taxation, was essential to overcoming mental deficiencies. Balanced nutrition that replaces junk foods with whole, plant-based foods is essential, along with adequate rest to have a healthy mind. This was sounding more and more like farm life!

We began to see that there is a place for programs. Our children were definitely benefited by the *Brighter Futures* program. But if the programs are not combined with a wholistic lifestyle—where there is a balance between the physical, mental, and spiritual—they fail to accomplish all they should.

The business was floundering, John was missing the farm and the children were missing their father. They did not want him to continue with *Brighter Futures*. I, on the other hand, struggled with giving up the *Brighter Futures* program. For the first eight months, the business had provided a small but steady income without my help. I really enjoyed that! But the children said they would rather have less money and work with their father on the farm. What could I say? With gratitude I embraced the reality that our children were not motivated by money. They missed the lifestyle the farm offered and longed to return to what they knew as "normal." Every indication led us to believe that we were to put our hand back on the plow and not look back. Why the detour into *Brighter Futures*? We may never understand completely; hindsight is not *always* 20/20 in this world.

Spring challenges

Spring was upon us and even though we were not "officially" involved with the strawberry crop, we managed the farm for five days while Edwin and Jennifer went away in early April. The field was full of flowers and green fruit and we were still in the season of damaging frost.

Trouble started on April 3. Out-of-state friends visited and at worship time we shared some of the experiences God had brought us through. We were just getting up from prayer when it came: High winds made us wonder if we should run to the root cellar. Then the hail came. It was a pounding hail that sounded like rocks falling on the roof. We dropped back to our knees, pleading for mercy. The hail was so loud that most of us just prayed in our hearts. Incredibly, no loss was sustained!

For the next five nights we covered the berries and frost protected every night. Two of those nights the temperature was down to 15 and 18 degrees in the field! This was a devastating freeze which destroyed most of the fruit and berries in the whole state, but God spared our berries! Because of our experience, and our proximity to the field, we continued to help with the frost protection even after Edwin and Jennifer returned.

The weather was wonderful until April 15 which is the average "last frost" date. All of the covers had been taken out of the field because we thought that frost protection was over for the season. But temperatures started dropping again. Not long after midnight John went out to put the sprinklers on. The valve broke in a way that could not be fixed without a town trip and special tools. It was a long and wakeful night. We prayed often for God's mercies. John and I laid awake off and on for hours wondering if we should wake everyone up, get the covers out of the barn and put them back on the field. He finally decided that doing so might do more damage than good, and we relied on the Lord for protection. He was faithful!

The next day we made a serious mistake. We did not make it a top priority to get the pipe fixed. On Tuesday, the 17th, the temperatures started dropping again. Now we had a huge problem . . . no covers **and** no sprinklers. We spent a long and troublesome night chastising ourselves and wondering why the Lord hadn't impressed us to do something. This wasn't even our crop! How would we explain the loss to Edwin and Jennifer? We continued to wrestle with the Lord until we found peace. The next morning John went walking and asked the Lord what lesson he should learn from this experience. The answer was fast and clear—BE READY! What a vivid reminder of our constant need to focus on eternal realities! Jesus is coming . . . we must be ready!

I praise the Lord for a deeper level of peace and abiding. I have put in hours of help with the berries and God has given me peace about someone else earning the profits. I have peace though I have very little money.

John and Edwin left for Maine on the nineteenth to help the extended family build a log cabin at a youth camp in Stephen's memory. I made a big mistake—I didn't listen to the weather! At midnight the temperature was 38 and by 1:30 a.m. the alarm went off warning us that it was 34 degrees. Over the next four hours the temperature rose and fell. With each drop back to 34 degrees, the alarm sounded. At 5:30, I awoke to a temperature of 32 degrees in the field. I went out to start the sprinklers and found the system hooked up for drip irrigating instead of frost protecting. I ran up to the house and called Jonathan to come. By 5:45 we had the sprinklers protecting the crop. Some damage was sustained, but it was minimal compared to what might have been. We gave thanks.

That year the strawberries were early. By the time John and Edwin left for Maine we were already picking berries. Surprisingly, one of the largest pickings of the season happened while they were gone. Those were busy days! We had a lot of peace, but we also had some faint-hearted moments. Financial stresses just kept increasing. God had done a mighty work of peace in my heart, yet I still struggled to face the money shortages. When I went to the pantry, did laundry, or sat at my desk, I was reminded of our dire straits. I longed to be at total and perfect rest, no matter what!

May 7, 2007

Father, You are all I need! I know You love me though I can get "intense" and speak my mind. You know the hurt. You know the desire in my heart for change. You know it all. I desire to be whole! To experience perfect peace. To express myself to others in a way that doesn't put them on the defensive. . . . I don't want to make excuses, but it is hard not to be intense. My life is that way. Bills to pay, no money, overwork . . . child training challenges.

A quiet stream. That's what I long to be. Cool . . . refreshing . . . meek . . . unpretentious. Lord, I have not overcome my irritable spirit. Grief of all griefs, I have passed this terrible trait of character on to my children. Pain of all pains, to stamp my children with a character trait that they now must overcome because I haven't!

We are more than a week overdue in paying our mortgage. I just received a call from a bill-collecting agency over something I thought I paid in full but they say we owe $600. Our insurance payment of $342 is due in two weeks. We usually pay for our World Vision sponsorship ($360) in June. On top of that there is our unfinished house. Lord show me how to approach life in a calm and peaceful way. When I feel the intensity all around, You are calling me to peace. I can safely rest knowing that You have a plan. Thank You for giving me a heart to serve and help with the strawberry crop. Three long days a week I am helping customers, managing orders, and picking berries. You have given peace and I trust that You have all our financial needs on Your heart.

God answered my prayers. I had moments of unrest, but overall He was giving me victory and reminding me that He would be faithful to supply our need.

This year, for the first time in our experience, cedar waxwings and opossums stole the last part of the berry crop. The birds came by day and the opossums by night. We knew farmers who were shooting the birds and carrying them out of their fields in five-gallon bucket. In the end, I'm not sure they fared any better than we did. When they killed one bird, two would take its place.

God has a thousand ways to provide for us, of which we know nothing!

With no income, we struggled constantly. *Brighter Futures* provided a little bit here and there, but nothing we could count on. We had a good-sized mortgage payment that was strangling us. At the end of March, I had no idea how we would make our April payment. For once, I wasn't concerned. God was giving me the victory over fear, and it was exhilarating to experience a more consistent rest relating to the finances. We just kept praying and asking God to provide what we needed. The answer came in a most unexpected way.

One of our neighbors called. She had just totaled her Toyota Previa minivan. These vans are old and hard to find. The neighbor's young passenger remembered seeing our old Previa with the blown head gasket sitting in a barn on our place. Would we be willing to sell it? *Would* we! This was just the answer we needed! Not only did the van cover our mortgage for that month, but there was a little left for other necessities. We reveled in God's goodness! We had never even thought of the old van as a means for providing needed funds!

In spite of our best efforts, the strawberry crop didn't yield as well as it should have. The children had hoped to use their earnings for a mission trip but there wasn't enough money to do that. Disappointment over poor crops was something we understood, but it was harder to see our children and extended family experience such difficulties.

Our immediate family was at an all-time low financially. All our efforts to build up *Brighter Futures* had failed. We felt God leading us back to full-time farming. We recommitted to be faithful to our calling, trusting that the farm was to be our "Brighter Future."

CHAPTER 14

Empty Pockets & Peace

SUMMER 2007–SPRING 2008

"You will keep him in perfect peace, whose mind is stayed on You: because he trusts in You" (Isaiah 26:3). "The Lord will give strength to His people; The Lord will bless His people with peace" (Psalm 29:11). We were tasting this peace, though nothing about our circumstances seemed much different. God allowed trials of a different sort to touch our lives this year. This time our children were the brunt of the devil's attacks.

July 26, 2007: Time out by the creek

I LOVE the creeks! So many lessons to be learned. I long for my life to be like a babbling brook. So often I feel like a stagnant pool, focused on the muck and mire. The very thing that makes the creek so beautiful—the rocks—could represent my trials. Without rocks the creek doesn't babble, but those rocks give it a song to sing. So also my trials can give me a voice of praise or a cry of despair. The creek can be cheerful and soothing, or rush like a mighty river after a heavy rainfall.

Father, carry me. I feel too weak to stand. Every meal on the table is a blessing from You. Help me to focus on what's on the table not what isn't in the pantry. Give us wisdom to know our part to solve our situation. Please send your Holy Spirit to speak to me through Your Word.

"I would have lost heart, unless I had believed that I would see the goodness of the LORD in the land of the living. Wait on the LORD, be of good courage, And He shall strengthen your heart, wait I say on the LORD" (Psalm 27:13, 14).

"The LORD will bless His people with peace" (Psalm 29:11).

I am His so I claim that peace. I feel that peace and thank You for helping me to focus on the "haves" not the "have nots." I go home with renewed strength to conquer the work that lies nearest.

Boy sized trials

Jonathan and Joshua decided to grow a half acre of sweet corn. That's more work than most twelve and fourteen year old boys are willing to tackle. But hard, manly work is exactly what boys need, so we encouraged their venture. Early in the spring they plowed the field and planted the seed. Next they faithfully cultivated the crop. It gave us great joy to see the many hours of sweat equity they poured into that crop. Our boys matured right along with the corn. The crop looked excellent and the boys began dreaming of the ways they would spend their hard-earned profits.

Just as the corn was ripening, word spread throughout the raccoon population that dinner was served! At the first sign of damage, we encouraged the boys, along with two lazy dogs we were "dog-sitting," to sleep out in the field. Unfortunately, that is just what they all did. They slept! For three weeks, dogs and boys **slept** while the coons crept in, night after night, and escaped with the fruits of their labor. Sitting on the porch with several dozen coon-damaged ears, the boys expressed their disappointment and frustration. They handled it like men—and faithful men at that. They never blamed God for this disappointment—which boosted our own courage.

While the boys wrestled with the dismal corn crop, John, Kirsten, and I started looking for solutions to the growing wild animal problem. We felt sure that dogs were the solution so we began an intense exploration of different breeds. We decided that Karelian Bear Dogs were the best choice. Unfortunately, there were very few Karelian breeders in the States.

We "stumbled" across a breeder in Washington State the very first day their website was up. The site belonged to someone of our faith who had gone to school with my sister-in-law! We had close friends who lived in Washington near this breeder. These friends were moving back to Tennessee at the very time the puppy would be ready to adopt. It all seemed providential. The only fly in the ointment was the fact that we didn't have any money for a dog.

After much prayer, we decided to use the children's hard-earned mission money for dogs. We hoped that the first litter of puppies would pay back, and hopefully multiply, their funds. We looked forward to a family mission trip. Planning even farther into the future, we decided that we would use the profit from future litters of puppies to pay down our mortgage. Arrangements were made. Near the beginning of August our friends brought the cutest little puppy! Klair Bear was her name. Joshua was the proud "owner," but we all fell in love with her. Quickly it was clear that she was the answer to our wild animal problems.

Negotiating with the Lord

"Not unto us, O Lord, not unto us, but to Your name give glory, Because of Your truth. Why should the Gentiles say, 'so where is their God?'" (Psalm. 115:1, 2).

"Ask, and it will be given to you. . . . For everyone who asks receives" (Matthew 7:7).

Father, Friend, Companion, Guide, Comfort, and Peace, we have sought You and You have been found. We have knocked and the doors have opened. We have asked and You have given. The last couple of months, actually many months, have been a peaceful hand-to-mouth existence. I praise You for the peace in my heart. I really do trust that somehow You are working all out for our good. You have been so patient with me and slowly I am learning.

Recently, I was struck by the fact that, if we had continued teaching, we would now be debt free—living a comfortable life in the cabin. But Your way has been perfect for our family. We know You have led us through the wilderness and we are coming forth conquerors through Christ. . . .

I sat down with our finances and realized that we still have 170 payments on our mortgage. Without Your help and intervention, we will be living a hand-to-mouth existence for the next fifteen or more years! I laid my hands on those papers and asked You to take care of it. We have done our best to follow You, though I know we've made many mistakes. Doing Your will is more important to us than having the things of this world. For ten years You have taught us and trained us by trial and error (on our part).

So what I want to ask (not my will but Thine be done) is for some back salary. That seems reasonable to me, so here is the dollar amount so far as I am able to figure it out [and I gave a number]. I'm asking for you to give us that much in back wages. . . . You are a good Master and I know You delight to give good gifts to Your children. Give me faith to believe that You will, in one of Your thousand ways, clear this debt. We will give You all the honor, glory and praise.

Forever Yours—with or without debt

In August and September the work load was especially heavy as we prepared for the winter season. There were strawberries to propagate, fields to prepare, transplants to set out. We enjoyed working with Edwin and Jennifer, anticipating and planning for our first winter CSA together. John was thrilled to be out of the office and back on the farm. The children were becoming a real asset to the farm. We thoroughly enjoyed working together.

In the fall, Edwin and Jennifer's oldest daughter moved to our area with her family. Evangeline's husband had a job transfer that moved them from Northern California to Spring Hill, just thirty minutes from our farm! They started looking for a spot to build on Edwin and Jennifer's property, but Edwin asked if they would like to purchase the log cabin. They loved the cabin and felt it was all they wanted and needed at that point. We were all thankful and believed that God worked things out in the best way possible.

October 22, 2007

Father, Your blessings are ever flowing and I pray that I can keep those thoughts fresh in my mind. I want to focus on Your goodness and care, but sometimes I focus on my "losses." Yesterday was one of those times. I went to greet Evie and see how the moving in was going. I'm not sure what hit me, but without warning, I just broke down and cried. All the memories, hopes, and dreams came flooding over me. Evie was very understanding. She held me in her arms while we cried together. What a precious, understanding woman she has become. It happened again when I told John about it. The hot tears streamed down my face. But Father, You know and I know that I'm okay and it will be okay. Evie and Cheyenne love the house. . . . You are my help when life looks hard or disappointing, You give me the ability to focus on eternal realities.

October 25, 2007

Dear Lord,

I'm back again, feeling that the financial burdens are going to crush us. "We don't know what to do, but our eyes are upon You." [From one of our favorite stories found in 2 Chronicles 20.] Lord, we've tried to follow Your leading. And where has it gotten us? We are in abject poverty—with a lot of debt and not a penny in savings. We're not asking for riches, but we do need Your help to get out of this mess. The farm seems to be sapping all our time and energy and we are not getting enough in return to even cover our basic living expenses. Somehow this doesn't seem to be the picture of someone being blessed by the Lord. Yes, I'm sure we've made mistakes—but they've been honest ones! Give us wisdom and strength to know and do our part and faith to trust You to do Yours.

The fall was a tough time. We were still recovering from the financial loss of the previous year. *Brighter Futures* was no longer providing us with any income. It takes time for a farm to increase production to provide for two families. But it is always at the low times that God is the nearest, and our eyes were fixed on Him. The farm was paying us a small salary, but not enough to cover our basic needs plus our loan. Things were getting desperate.

November 1, 2007

We are in a seemingly hopeless position. But, I choose not to address that. I just give it to You. Father, if You want us to be debt free, then I know You'll make it a reality. But, if we are to live in dire poverty for the rest of our lives, I'm willing. Heaven is cheap enough, and if this is what it takes for me, I'm willing. (Make me willing when I'm not.)

Because we have a High Priest who can sympathize with our weakness, I am invited to come BOLDY to the throne of grace, to obtain mercy and find grace to help in time of need (Hebrews 4:15, 16).

Father, I feel it's the same old theme I bring before You again and again. I have boldly asked for two things:

1. Peace amid any type of material or financial crisis.
2. Deliverance from the debt that we have incurred by our efforts to follow Your plan for our lives.

Father, I ask for faith! Please, give me faith to know that You will deliver.

These days were intense. With more family around, it was increasingly difficult to hide our financial distress. Many times we would find a little cash with a note on our table, or someone would clean out their pantry of "excess food" and ask us to help them use it. We still chose to talk faith, and we never told anyone about our "want," so we accepted these gifts as tokens of God's love.

Good morning Father,

What an unexpected blessing to be alone with You for hours. You must have known that I needed this. I cherish this extra time alone! Our daily date is great, but these bonus times always go too fast. What message have You prepared for me? Wow, that's an amazing thought that You have prepared a word for me. May self be put aside and may You empty my mind of other thoughts that I may focus on You speaking to my heart. . . .

"Then the LORD will be zealous for His land, And pity His people. . . . Behold, I will send you grain and new wine and oil, And you will be satisfied by them. . . . So I will restore to you the years that the swarming locust has eaten. . . . You shall eat in plenty and be satisfied, And praise the name of the LORD your God, Who has dealt wondrously with you; And My people shall never be put to shame" (Joel 2).

What beautiful promises! I believe You want to "restore the years the locust have eaten." How and when? These are not mine to know. It is mine to trust!

What peace there is in the presence of Jesus! I came away from that "High Sabbath" feeling like God had given me His word and that He was to be trusted. The blessings came in big and small packages through the winter, and as we continually looked to the Lord, we had peace that passed our own understanding.

Family and farm life

Apart from the financial stresses, our family was characterized by positive attitudes and a love for the life we were called to live. Our children were almost always willing workers—it was just the way of life and they loved it. Of course we did have our share of parenting challenges, but we saw good "fruit" from living a life on the land! Our children developed a strong work ethic, could push through on tough jobs, and learned the joy and satisfaction of a job well done. Building our barn house was a tremendous learning experience for the boys. No, it wasn't finished, but we kept working on it. Jonathan and Joshua participated in every part of the construction. Kirsten pitched right in and helped wherever she could. They all learned how to use power tools, build shelving, paint, clean up the job site, and ever so many other practical skills. We were now quite comfortable in the house and looked forward to finishing the work. But the biggest priority was the farm. We had to get production up enough to provide comfortably for two families.

QUIET AND SIMPLE

"The more quiet and simple the life of the child,—the more free from artificial excitement, and the more in harmony with nature,—the more favorable is it to physical and mental vigor and to spiritual strength" (Ellen White, *The Desire of Ages*, p. 74).

Any "success" we have had in parenting is due to following this counsel. At the beginning, we committed to making this quote our motto. Our efforts have been imperfect at best, but God has blessed our attempts to follow His ways.

Our modern society seems to be diametrically opposed to this statement; children's lives are loud and complicated, artificial excitement is everywhere, and nature is something viewed on a television channel. Early childhood education proponents encourage parents to fill their children's lives with extracurricular activities: sports, music, arts, parties, and the list goes on. Television, computers, and video games are encouraged as "educational" and important to future success. From our vantage point, we strongly disagree; it's largely just artificial excitement.

When we took up farming, the economic realities "forced" us to this quiet and simple life, but what a blessing! Our testimony is that children are more content, more creative, and more open to counsel if artificial excitement is avoided. Nature has a calming effect, and God is more readily able to teach them when they are surrounded by the things He made. Following God's counsel may not produce child prodigies; growth in nature is usually slow and steady, but the fruit is sweet for those who are patient.

We challenge you to swim against the current of the world. Put this statement to the test; positive results are guaranteed!

Having Edwin and Jennifer here to share the burden was a real blessing. Together we made plans for the future of our farm. They contributed additional finances to add hoop houses and other equipment for increased productivity. The CSA was bigger than it had ever been and the customers were very happy with the produce. Contact with the customers kept me inspired and motivated to push forward on hard days. Our customers frequently shared testimonials about improved health through the winter months since they became a part of our CSA. Such encouragement gave us courage and made the heavy load a bit lighter.

Bear dogs

We had all fallen in love with Klair Bear. She grew into a beautiful dog and we started looking for a mate. The Lord led us to a man in South Dakota who had a one-and-a-half year old male for sale. The dog was from good stock and had different blood lines. We felt sure he was the mate for Klair. In early May—just as the strawberries were in full production—we went to the Nashville airport and picked up Trail Blazer. When he crawled out of the crate, he just seemed to get bigger and bigger. Klair was mid-sized, but Blazer weighed in at seventy-five pounds and stood several inches taller.

From the very first, Klair and Blazer seemed to know they belonged together. They immediately became hunting companions. At first we'd hear them chasing and barking, doing just what they were born to do. Soon Blazer would get weary and go to sleep in the shade of the barn. But not Klair! She didn't seem to know the word defeat. She stayed out in the fields, rooting out moles by the hours. Her greatest show of determination came when she and Blazer treed a groundhog. How that groundhog got up in the tree we will never know, but we heard Klair and Blazer barking furiously. The children went to investigate and brought back the report about the poor, treed groundhog. After an hour or two, Blazer retired to the shade. Klair sat at the base of that tree barking for the next seven hours! Exhausted and hoarse, she retreated to the barn for a hasty meal. Returning to the tree, she discovered that the groundhog had made his escape while he could. We found Klair whining and whimpering at the base of the tree some hours later. I am sure that groundhog spread the word about our "ferocious" bear dogs and never set his paws on our farm again!

In an attempt to improve our financial outlook, we decided to close the field for u-pick. That was a difficult decision for our family. After ten years, we had built many relationships with customers through the u-pick, and we realized that many of our friends might not make the transition from picking their own strawberries to buying them already picked. Hard as the decision was, we all felt that this was a necessary step.

Now that the customers were no longer picking their own berries, we had the added work of picking all of them ourselves. Then we had to find customers to purchase them. This was a faith-walk, as I am the one who gets orders and finds sales—after I'm done picking that is! We try to sell everything on the day it's picked. Many, many times I looked at dozens of flats of berries and wondered how and where we were going to sell them all! But, we always did, and my faith and confidence in God were always increased.

Spring is always a busy time of year, but that year it got even busier. My niece and nephew came to stay with us for two weeks. Company is always fun, but this time someone brought an illness that changed the course of our summer.

CHAPTER 15

It's the Darkest Just Before Dawn

SUMMER–FALL 2008

At first, it seemed like a simple summer cold going around our house, so I didn't take it too seriously. Jonathan came down with it, but in his usual fashion, he was back up and working in a couple of days. *It's impossible to keep Jonathan down*, I thought. A week later, after the company had gone, Jonathan came to me one afternoon complaining that his ear was throbbing. Soon he was in excruciating pain. My efforts to bring relief failed. I consulted with my father-in-law, who is our "family doctor." He told me to try and make my son comfortable, and wait. In the middle of the night, the eardrum ruptured and Jonathan finally felt some relief. The next day we took him to the doctor who put him on antibiotics. He didn't improve. Jonathan slept for almost five days straight, hardly eating or drinking anything. We were heading into our most challenging summer and miraculous fall.

At the same time, Klair Bear started limping. We assumed she had injured her paw but we could not see anything. Then one of her eyes became cloudy. We took her to the vet and she tested positive for a tick-borne disease. Soon Klair was on antibiotics. She was Joshua's dog and he took her condition very seriously. Daily we prayed over her, asking the Lord to heal her. We believed He would; wasn't she our mission dog? Hadn't God miraculously brought her into our family?

Jonathan was sick, Klair was sick, and we were preparing for a fiftieth anniversary celebration for John's parents. The family gathering gave us the added medical counsel of John's brother, Wayne, who is a physician. After examining Jonathan, he told us he thought we were doing everything we could, but that he had been much sicker than we had realized. It would take time for him to recover. This seemed so strange to us! Jonathan has always had an excellent immune system. He rarely got sick, and rebounded amazingly fast. After eight days with this "bug" he was still lethargic, sleepy, and lacking in appetite. The celebration for my in-laws included a much anticipated, week-long vacation to Edisto Island. It was decided that Jonathan's slow-but-steady recovery could continue as well, or maybe even better at the beach.

The long trip to South Carolina left Jonathan exhausted. Just sitting up in the car wore him out. When we got settled in our beach house, he went straight to bed. After a good night's sleep, he thought he would like to go to the beach. We were thrilled. We walked the couple of blocks with him, hoping that the fresh breeze would energize him. After only a few minutes, Jonathan asked me to walk him back to the house. I watched him moving along so slowly and my heart ached to fix whatever was wrong. *How could it be*, I asked myself, *that my strong, active, healthy son had become so feeble and sickly?*

June 18, 2008

Good morning, Father,

Thank You for the cool of the morning, for the bird songs and all of nature that draws me to You. The lack of human distractions makes it easy to turn my thoughts to You. What a blessing this family time is! The rest and relaxation is exactly what we have been needing and looking forward to.

Father, today is the tenth day in a row that Jonathan has been sick. I ask You to place Your healing hand on him, to give him strength, and renew his energy. If there is any other thing going on in his body, I pray You will give us wisdom to know if we need to check it out. If it's just rest he needs, then I pray he will continue to show progress. Give Dad and Wayne wisdom to know if there is something more that needs to be done. I would just ask that You place Your healing hand on him so that he can take part in the reunion and enjoy the beach. It's been hard for us to see him being the observer, not the life of the party. Touch him I pray.

On the second day at the beach, Jonathan told me his vision was blurry. Not being a medical person, and being a non-alarmist, I didn't think too much about it. When Wayne heard about this, he came straight to John and me and told us that if Jonathan was his son, he would take him to the emergency room. We left immediately.

It was no coincidence that we were vacationing close to one of the best children's hospitals in the country. We arrived at the emergency room at 6:30 p.m. Amazingly, it was empty. We were grateful for the unexpected peace and quiet as we waited to see a doctor. John, Dad, Wayne, and I sat looking at Jonathan and marveling that he "looked" so normal. In some ways he seemed to be improving, but the blurred vision made Wayne believe that there was a deeper issue.

The ER may have been empty, but it was still a long night. Initial blood work looked good. No signs of infection. My brother-in-law kept coming back to the fact that the blurred vision was the real concern and they needed to figure out the cause. A CT scan was ordered. By this time it was midnight and we were all exhausted. The doctor reported that the CT scan looked good, but he wanted us to wait for the radiologist to read it before he let us go. We tried to persuade him otherwise, stating that he could call us with the results, but he insisted that we stay. We waited. We waited some more. During those long hours, we had plenty of time to talk. We learned that this was Wayne's first time in an emergency room since his son Stephen's death. How strange and sad that he was here with Jonathan who was now the same age Stephen was when he died. I didn't allow myself to dwell on these thoughts too much.

Around 2:00 a.m. we finally got the radiology report. There was a blockage in the transverse sinus vein, the main vein which drains blood from the brain. An MRI was ordered to further assess the situation.

Medical personnel rattled off a diagnosis, but most of us had no idea what it meant. Wayne asked them to print out some information for us. I watched the concern on the faces of the men as they read and whispered among themselves. It seems that 80 percent of people with this diagnosis died. I did not read the printout. I just prayed!

At 3:30 a.m., Jonathan was wheeled in for the MRI. The TV in the waiting room was on and I was forced to listen to interviews of families who had lost loved ones to septicemia. Septicemia! That was Jonathan's diagnosis twelve days after birth! But instead of upsetting me, this thought brought comfort. I felt the Lord assuring me that, in the same way He had spared Jonathan's life then, He would spare it now.

The results of the MRI confirmed our concerns. The right transverse sinus vein was totally blocked with blood clots. The resulting pressure was causing the blurred vision. Spinal fluid pressure was nearly double what it should have been. Somewhere around this time we got word that the ER's diagnosis was not correct. Jonathan was still a very sick young man, but he was not under a diagnosis that had an 80 percent mortality rate!

It was 5:00 a.m. when they wheeled Jonathan into a hospital room. We dropped onto whatever bed and chair space we could find. We were utterly exhausted but we hadn't been there more than ten minutes when interns started arriving. Five different specialists were assigned to Jonathan's case. Word was out that there was an unusual case on the fourth floor. Every one of those specialists, and a host of support staff came and went. Each one wanted to check the same things and ask the same questions. By the fifth interruption my motherly instinct kicked in and I said, "Enough is enough! Jonathan needs some rest! Please don't disturb us again!"

Over time we began to understand the chain of events that brought us to this place. Jonathan hadn't caught a summer cold. He had a strep infection. It worked its way into an inner-ear infection, which then progressed to a massive mastoid infection. The mastoiditis caused the blood clot, which led to blurred vision, which led us to the ER. Despite the fact that his blood work looked good, Jonathan was dangerously ill!

The first step was surgery, which was scheduled for early that afternoon.

June 20, 2008

Father, You know all. From the "cold" to surgery. Again I fully surrender Jonathan's life into Your hands. You are in control. It was extremely difficult to see them wheel him away from us into surgery. Now as we wait, we roll our anxious thoughts onto Your broad shoulders. Thank You for carrying us during difficult times and sustaining us with Your peace.

The five-hour surgery went well. We felt so thankful for the care Jonathan received. The doctor did his best to remove the infected bone and tissue. He even tried to remove some of the clot from the vein. The infection was so severe that, according to the physician, the mastoid bone was like "soaked Rice Krispies"—totally mush from infection. We prayed that the blood would begin to flow through that vein so he wouldn't need more serious interventions - like a brain shunt.

Every other day Jonathan endured a spinal tap to keep the increased pressure under control. Every doctor who saw him was amazed that he didn't have a splitting headache. One day Jonathan looked at me in frustration and exclaimed, "What is a headache? Maybe I do have one!"

Jonathan's patience humbled me. Imagine telling a fourteen-year-old boy to lay still and not move for forty-five minutes! But over and over again he did it. His pain tolerance amazed all of his caregivers. Spinal tap after spinal tap, MRI after MRI, shot after shot, he took it all without a complaint. I believe that good nutrition, manual labor, plenty of fresh air, and lots of sunshine had made him strong physically and emotionally. Never did he complain. Not once did he say, "Why me?"

Faith grows in many ways. We were again being stretched. The Lord impressed on my heart the thought that we were not just in that hospital to receive a blessing, but also to be a blessing. So each morning we prayed, "Lord make us a blessing to someone today." The doctors were still trying to understand what, exactly, was going on with Jonathan. How could he have such a major illness, yet show so few symptoms? How could they get the spinal pressure to stay down? Six doctors and interns were standing in his room one morning perplexed at how to proceed. I mustered the courage to say something to them.

"Jonathan's case is a good reminder of the fact that we don't have all the answers," I said. "We must go to the One who created the body. We're praying every day that God will give you wisdom to know just what to do." I don't know what the doctors thought of my little speech, but I felt it was important for them to know that they were receiving help from a Mind wiser than their own.

On the fifth day of our stay, John and the family had to return to the farm. We hated being apart! I hugged all the children, trying to be strong for them. Caleb's parting words to me were, "Mommy, my ear hurts." *Oh no, not another earache!* My typically non-alarmist self told John he'd better get Caleb to the doctor as soon as they got home. Never again would we take an earache lightly!

June 25, 2008

Father, You are so good! These trials are hitting on our children's level and I believe You are strengthening their faith. It has been a rough day, yet with You by our sides, there is peace. We got the news this morning that Klair has Blastomycosis—no medical cure!

I shed quite a few tears as I thought of losing her. . . . It's hard because of the miraculous way we found her and got her. So that has been a hard thing—but not as hard as the news of Caleb. John took him to the doctor and he tested positive for strep, has an ear infection, and a heart murmur we knew nothing about. John is now at Vanderbilt in the ER with him trying to determine the cause of the murmur [they eventually determined it was a heart defect that he was born with, and was nothing to worry about]. Father, You know all and I truly trust You. I know You see the big picture that we don't see and if we did see it, we would not wish our situation to be ordered in any different way. I know that You have our eternal good in mind.

It was wonderful to hear Joshua's voice this evening. With joy and happiness spilling out, he explained how he felt Klair was doing better. Kirsten did some research on natural remedies. Following her directions, Klair had eaten some yogurt and dog food this morning. It also gave me joy to hear him express his faith in Your desire to save Klair based on the fact that she is our mission investment dog. Father,

I thank You for peace. You are the only one who could have given it to me today! I praise Your name!

Jonathan's body was slowly healing. The spinal pressure gradually came down. His vision improved slightly, although he was still seeing double. The scans of his brain showed the auxiliary veins enlarging to compensate for the vein that remained blocked. Plans were laid for our discharge and the twelve-hour trip home.

◇◇◇◇◇◇◇◇◇◇◇◇◇◇◇◇◇◇◇◇◇◇◇ *Sabbath, June 28, 2008* ◇◇◇◇◇◇◇◇◇◇◇◇◇◇◇◇◇◇◇◇◇◇◇

Good morning, Father,

Thank You for the rest of the night. Father, You are so good and so powerful to save. Yesterday, I felt Your sustaining hand. I know that You carried me and lifted me up during the whole day. I have found Your strength sufficient for me in weakness. Yesterday, I kept thinking of the song "Bow the Knee."

There are moments on our journey following the Lord,
where God illumines every step we take.
There are times when circumstances make perfect sense to us,
as we try to understand each move He makes.
When the path grows dim and our questions have no answers, turn to Him.

Bow the knee; Trust the heart of your Father when the answer goes beyond what
you can see.
Bow the knee; Lift your eyes toward heaven and believe the One who holds eternity.
And when you don't understand the purpose of His plan,
In the presence of the King, bow the knee.

There are days when clouds surround us, and the rain begins to fall,
the cold and lonely winds won't cease to blow.
And there seems to be no reason for the suffering we feel;
we are tempted to believe God does not know.
When the storms arise, don't forget we live by faith and not by sight.

*Bow the knee; Trust the heart of your Father when the answer goes beyond what
you can see.*
Bow the knee; Lift your eyes toward heaven and believe the One who holds eternity.
And when you don't understand the purpose of His plan,
In the presence of the King, Bow the knee;

—Words and music by Chris Machen and Mike Harland

No matter what happens around me, I long to be totally trusting of Your plan.
I know I can't get that experience; only You can give it to me. I just praise You for
peace. I continue to ask You for a miracle with Klair. Father, You know that we used
the children's mission money to purchase the dogs. . . . You know we've been wanting to go on a family mission trip and were counting on money from her puppies. If
she lives it will be because You touched her. Oh Father, what a powerful testimony
to our children; and how that would strengthen their faith! But, I realize only You
know what is best, so I "Bow the knee" and ask You to do what in Your all-knowing
wisdom is best!

Sunday morning, June 29, Jonathan was discharged. We were
shown how to administer shots and antibiotics. Then we began the
long trip home. Jonathan was still very sick and on heavy medications.
Once on the road, we called to let the family know we were on our way.
We were anxious to be reunited! The news from the other end took all
the wind out of our sails. Klair was dead.

I couldn't believe it! The floodgates of all my pent-up feelings
broke loose. All the tears I had not cried over the course of the last
few weeks just came streaming down. If I hadn't been so desperate to
get home, I would have pulled over and stopped. But we had to keep
going. Jonathan needed to get into his own bed. Through the tears, we
slowly made our way home. Home, where everything would be okay
once we were reunited. Home, where I could cry with my children over
the losses, the fears, and the trials. Most of all, we were going home to
the place where we could band together and accept by faith the things
we couldn't change.

After an hour of "bawling like a baby," my tears dried up and I began to focus on the blessings. Praise God it was not Jonathan who had died! He was a miracle boy! Such rare cases often leave physicians unsure about a treatment plan. But the Lord blessed us with doctors who were not afraid to admit that they were in need of Divine wisdom. The fact that Jonathan suffered no permanent vision or hearing loss was unexplainable. The head of Pediatric Ophthalmology had only seen five cases like Jonathan's in his career. He told us that Jonathan's optic nerves were the most stressed of the five cases, yet his vision was the best. He went on to say that in the other five cases they had to do eye surgery, with varying levels of success. Praise God for His mercy!

Reuniting with our family after any time apart is pure joy. We give due weight to the fact that separation does not always end with reunion. There is so much to tell one another, whether we've been apart a day or, as in this case, six days. We got Jonathan upstairs, then sat around his bed talking about the events of the last week. I held Caleb in my arms, feeling such gratitude that he was okay and that the heart issue was nothing to worry about.

Tucking Joshua in bed that night, we talked about Klair and how his faith was holding up. He said he didn't blame Jesus. He was just thankful that his prayers had been answered. He said that he prayed on Sabbath that he could see Klair wag that cute little tail one more time. That evening, she gave one last wag of her white-tipped tail. It was the way she showed her love for him. He went on to tell that he prayed again before he went to bed. He asked that if Klair was not going to be healed, that she would die that night. "Mommy," Joshua said, "Jesus answered my prayers!"

Oh yes, he was going to miss Klair terribly, as we all would. But his faith was strong. Praise God!

Making the rounds, I went to Kirsten. She had shouldered the home responsibilities while I was gone. It was difficult for her to be home alone with Joshua as Klair continued to worsen. John was with Caleb at the hospital that day, and I was far away in South Carolina with Jonathan. Kirsten felt the weight of the responsibilities that rested on her. I asked about how her faith held up during that time and she immediately assured me that she trusted in Jesus to see her through. Again my heart was full of gratitude! Faith was what we wanted, not just for ourselves, but for our children. Faith is what we have to hold onto when we can't solve our own problems. Each of our children was hit with severe personal trials that summer and every one of them chose to trust!

The next morning John dug a deep hole for Klair. As he carried her to it, our tears flowed freely. She was our mission investment. She was our human effort to add a little to our mortgage repayment fund. She was our hunter. She was an answer to our prayers. As John knelt down to lay her in the hole, Blazer came and licked Klair's nose. Then he went around the hole and, with his nose, pushed dirt in on her. The tears *still* flow whenever I recount it. Completing the circle, Blazer sat down and looked up at us as if to say, "I've done my part, now you can finish the job." Gathering around that fresh mound of dirt, we lifted our hearts in prayer. We asked God to make us faithful whether we could understand life's trials or not. God *was* in control, and though we didn't understand, we chose to believe that these experiences had eternal value.

It was a long summer and a very slow recovery for Jonathan. He continued for six more weeks on heavy antibiotics, home health visits, and shots twice a day. Not once did he swim, get on his bike, or drive the tractor. Only once do I remember him complaining.

By his birthday in August, Jonathan was getting back to being his normal self. In October, we discontinued the blood-thinning shots. We have much gratitude for God's protecting and healing hand!

Apprenticeship program begins

It was during that fall, just about the time we started propagating the strawberries, that we launched our apprenticeship program. In retrospect, we were not at all ready for this step, but despite our limitations, God chose to use us.

We got a phone call. The caller had a daughter who wanted to learn about gardening. Would we consider having her come and learn on the farm? We prayerfully agreed. Since we had one "student," Edwin decided that his children, Caroline and Paul, might benefit from taking the classes. These three, along with Kirsten, made up our first class. It was a life changing experience for all. Kirsten went from being a farmer's daughter to being a farmer. Her eyes were opened to the deeper value of the life we lived. Ever since that time she has been united with us in our passion for an agrarian life of ministry.

The fall rush was on. The strawberries were in and the crops were nearly ready to start the winter CSA. We hoped to have a larger group this year, but one thing we have learned is that God brings us what we can handle, not what we plan for.

God's radical call for our means

During our Africa years we were inspired by another missionary's example in the area of tithing. It was there we began the practice of giving a second tithe. While studying the Bible, we saw that this was God's plan for His people in the Old Testament. The second tithe was to help the poor, particularly to enable them to attend the religious festivals.

At the beginning of our marriage we covenanted with God to return a faithful 10 percent of our income as tithe, and 5 percent for offerings to our church. Then, in Kenya, we added the additional 10 percent so we would have money to help those in need. We believe that the poor are placed among us to check our selfishness. There are widows, orphans, and worthy poor in all of our lives. Then there are the various ministries, or charitable organizations that need our help. According to the Bible, the second tithe was to be held in the home every third year to support the ministry of hospitality.

We knew God's plan was not intended to impoverish us, but rather to strengthen our financial situation along with our spiritual depth. In the twelve years since John left teaching, we discovered that we would never have anything to use in blessing others if we did not faithfully carry out the biblical principle of setting aside God's portion first. After we instituted this practice, we usually had money to share when someone was in need. The problem was that we often felt like we were that "someone" in need. At times we had money to help others, while our own cupboards were "empty." Because of this, we sometimes felt the temptation to question this practice. We had grown inconsistent about giving the second tithe.

Now it was two years since we had faithfully given this second tithe. John and I were each convicted separately that we had broken a financial commitment with the Lord. Through the summer I had the best of intentions to hold the money back. But if I didn't get God's money out of the bank immediately, it would be gone, just in providing for the basic needs of our family. In September, I confessed to John that I had wanted to pay that extra tithe, but I just wasn't able to do it. Unintentionally, we had already used September's and it was only the middle of the month. "Do you think the Lord is really asking us to do this?" I questioned.

John thought about it a minute and said, "Honey, we are going to put the Lord to the test. For September, October, and November, we are going to pay the second tithe. If, at the end of that time, we see that we really can't make it, we will assume the Lord is freeing us from our commitment."

When I got our check for October, I immediately took out the 25 percent for tithes and offerings, plus the back second tithe for September. I put the cash away where it could not be accessed for paying the family's bills. I then paid the other bills. Now there was nothing left, but I can honestly testify that the Lord gave me perfect peace. I wasn't sure how it was going to work out, but we were taking the Malachi challenge, "Bring ye all the tithes into the storehouse, . . . and prove me now herewith, saith the Lord of hosts, if I will not open you the windows of heaven, and pour you out a blessing, that there shall not be room enough to receive it" (Malachi 3:10).

October of 2008 was a time of fear and uncertainty in America. Banks were closing, hundreds of thousands of people were losing their homes, and the economy was teetering on the edge of collapse. Most conversations were tinged with anxiety. We too were concerned.

Calling an emergency meeting with the extended farm family, we talked about how we could band together to weather the storm. Our greatest concern was the fact that our house loan was against the farm. This was a problem none of us could solve. We also talked of steps that we could take to become more independent from the world's systems. We finished our time together by listening to the president's emergency address to the nation. Going home, our minds were stirred with excitement, and with concerns about the immediate future.

I had a restful sleep but when I woke up I found John poring over catalogs. He said he had wakened from a vivid dream, and understood that we needed to prepare our farm for future hard times. He was also impressed to visit two people who might be willing to finance our mortgage. He asked me to make appointments with both of those people for that day. Heading into town that afternoon, we felt totally out of our comfort zone, but confident that the Lord was leading. The first contact said over and over that they were so grateful God had put them on our minds. We presented our request and asked that they pray about it. We had such a wonderful visit and went away knowing that God was guiding us. The second visit was equally enjoyable. Again we shared our concerns and the fact that we were looking for an individual to finance our home loan. We didn't know why the Lord had placed them on our hearts, but we were just following the impressions we had received. We left feeling at peace that we had followed the Lord's guidance.

The next morning I again awoke to find my husband out of bed and studying his Bible. It was October 16, and John had experienced another restless night. He shared that again God had impressed him to visit another individual about financing our mortgage. If John and I had sat down to make a list of people we would feel comfortable asking for a loan, we would not have chosen any that the Lord impressed us to visit. The very idea of asking was something we had covenanted never to do unless the Lord clearly and specifically led us to do so.

My husband usually thinks on things for a while before he acts. Not this time! As early as he felt it was appropriate, he called and asked if he could make an appointment with the third individual that day. Together we again went on the awkward errand. We were not as concerned with the outcome as with our obedience to the Lord's leading. We had a nice visit but, after laying out our request, we were told that no decision could be made until after the first of the year. We went away with perfect peace because we had followed God's lead.

Friday, October 17, we received an excited call from the individual we had visited the day before. In a miraculous way, God made it very clear to them that they were to help us. They had donated money to a charitable organization to purchase a piece of property. This organization called that morning to say the land purchase fell through, and they were wondering what they should do with the donated money. Our contact immediately told them to send it back. He knew just what he was going to do with it. He then went on to tell us that he and his wife had recently made the decision not to loan money any more. So, instead of a loan, they were just going to pay off our debt! Pay our debt? Could this be real? John was in shock as he heard the voice on the other end of the phone say. "The check will be in the mail tomorrow." The words "thank you" seemed so inadequate. We had just been emancipated; freed from the noose of debt! And it was not because of our "goodness," or because we had "earned" it; it was a gift! "Grace" took on a deeper meaning for us that day. Grace!

October 17, 2008

Dear Lord, our hearts are overflowing with gratitude this morning for your goodness and mercy. Today we learned that our debt is going to be paid in full! What can I say? I brought the family together and in trying to tell them the amazing news I just broke down and sobbed. You are so good! We thank You for taking us through these years of trial—where we have had to depend so completely upon You. I can already say that I wouldn't trade them for anything.

"This poor man cried out, and the Lord heard him, and saved him out of all his troubles" (Psalm 34:6). This is my testimony.

"O taste and see that the Lord is good. Blessed is the man that trusteth in Him" (Psalm 34:8). We have tasted and seen! You are good—debt or no debt!

We walked around in a daze, not able to believe the events of the day. What if John hadn't been willing to step out in faith? What if he hadn't followed the Lord's lead? What if we had reasoned away the impressions as foolishness? Or what if he was just too embarrassed to go forward? The Bible is true when it says, "And thine ears shall hear a word behind thee, saying, This is the way, walk ye in it, when ye turn to the right and when ye turn to the left" (Isaiah 30:21).

Eighteen months earlier I sat at my desk looking at that discouragingly long amortization schedule. I remember that the Lord impressed me right then that He was going to take care of our debt. On one of my High Sabbaths, He had brought me to the verses in Joel 2 and encouraged me that He was going to restore the years the locust had eaten. In September—just a few weeks before this miracle of freedom, we had taken the Malachi challenge and put the Lord to the test. Did He prove Himself faithful? The answer was crystal-clear. He truly opened the windows of Heaven and poured out His blessings—bountiful blessings!

We have tasted and seen that the Lord is good, but that goodness and those blessings are not for us alone. He will prove Himself faithful to you too!

"Here we raise our Ebenezer, hither by His help we've come."

To God be the glory!

Afterword

Our story has no good ending point, because there are new and exciting pages being written every day. God continues to lead and guide and bless at Bountiful Blessings Farm. Here are a few highlights from the intervening years.

Mission trip

It was just four months after our "emancipation" that we boarded a plane with nine other extended family members for our long-dreamed-about family mission trip. We had tried to make this happen through the children's strawberry crop and then through Klair Bear, but God made it a reality in His own time and way. It was amazing to watch the Lord bring the money together. We didn't ask anyone other than the Lord for help. He impressed hearts to give, with no help from us! God also knows how to stretch and multiply the little that we have. Edwin and Jennifer generously covered the farm for two weeks while we were gone.

We spent ten wonderful days doing Vacation Bible School with the children, presenting family and youth seminars, visiting people in their homes, and making sweet friendships with the church family in a little mountain village in Honduras. It was an amazing experience and a blessing to each one of us.

The farm

Bountiful Blessings Farm has continued to grow and mature through the years. In 2010, we started growing year round. This step seemed logical in order to maximize the use of our land and infrastructure, but going year round was difficult. Farmers, like strawberries, need a time of dormancy to rejuvenate! So, we divided the year, with Edwin's family managing the fall and winter months, and ours the spring and summer. This way our customers are ministered to year-round, while we each have a needed break. For a current update on the farm, see our website (www.bountifulblessingsfarm.com)

The Lord has blessed the fruits of our labor. We often hear how exceptional our produce is, and all we can do is give God the glory. Every crop is prayed over! We recognize our limitations and ask the Lord to do what we can't do: make the plants grow and fill them with nutrition and flavor. We will never get rich doing this, but we are now making a "living wage" from the farm. God continues to be our Senior Partner. There would be no Bountiful Blessings Farm without His leading and guiding!

Beyond farming, we enjoy teaching others through our apprenticeship programs, week-long seminars, weekend trainings, and one-day workshops. If you want to learn more about future training plans, keep an eye on our training website (www.bountifulblessingsshared.com). As God gives us opportunity to encourage others toward a more agrarian life, we aim to cooperate.

IN THE WORLD, BUT NOT OF IT

One of the most overlooked themes in the Bible, in my opinion, is the concept of separation from the world. From Genesis to Revelation, it is on almost every page and in every story. "Separation" is not politically correct. It smells of exclusiveness, prejudice, and bigotry, so we cozy up to the world and try not to stand out like a sore thumb.

We look with disdain on the children of Israel as they repeatedly chose to worship and intermarry with the heathen nations around them, but we are blind to the beam in our own eye (Matthew 7:3–5).

What does it mean to be separate from the world? I think it means we dress differently, we talk differently, we act differently, we eat differently, we sing differently, we educate differently, we live in the country, we "soil" our hands in the dirt, we "give" instead of "get," we walk by faith and not by sight (2 Corinthians 5:7).

Does this mean that we ignore the world and its problems? No! But we only "rub shoulders" when we have something to share. We are to be lights in the darkness, not sponges to soak up its customs and practices.

This concept may be labeled as fanatical, but I believe it's time for someone to stand up and say, "Stop sacrificing your children to Baal! Be different!" You can't send them to the world (or let them bring the world home on their devices), and expect that it is not going to affect them.

Farming and our family

Through the really tough years, I feared that the farm was too demanding, and our children would resent it. I took those fears to God—believing that I could trust His leading. I chose to believe that He would not allow the stern simplicity of farm life to destroy our children's love for an agrarian life. Placing the seed in the soil requires faith, and so does parenting. As we followed God, we were tempted in so many ways to think, *this is too hard!* But, I kept telling myself that there was no room for complaining about God's leading. I just needed to figure out how to make it work. Now my faith is stronger in every way. Farm life has been exactly what we all needed. Satan tempted us to question, but God called us to trust. Our children do not resent the lifestyle we chose in obedience to God's calling—they love and value it. Their own hopes for family and future are similar to what they grew up with. Here are some of Kirsten's thoughts that she shared during a seminar:

✴ ✴ ✴ ✴ ✴ *Thoughts from a Farm Girl* ✴ ✴ ✴ ✴ ✴
Kirsten Dysinger, age 16

The fact that I have grown up on a farm and am a farmer's daughter raises a lot of questions in peoples' minds. What was it like? What have you learned? What are some of the advantages and disadvantages? So, a few months ago, I wrote down my answers to some of these questions, and that's what Dad asked me to share today.

It's hard for me to come up with all the advantages, because, at least for me, there are so many! But here are a few:

Country living has really impacted my life. To have acres and acres of hills and forests to explore has been so much fun! And just being in nature is something we have all come to love and appreciate. When customers bring their children out to the farm, it is a little sad to hear them ask questions about some of the most basic things in nature. We are often told how "lucky" we are to live where we do, and have nature all around. It's a novelty to most, when it should be a God-given privilege more people enjoy.

Another blessing of farm life is hard work. Although I have not always viewed this as a blessing, I am coming to see that it really is, and now I actually enjoy it. Hard work is a concept most people, unfortunately, aren't acquainted with, and it is only to their downfall. There is plenty of hard work on a farm, and it is almost always coupled with a certain level of discomfort. Like being smothered beneath a massive raspberry jungle, in a sauna of a greenhouse, sweat pouring down your face, being pricked on all sides, etc. At the moment it may not seem like a blessing, but in the long run, it proves to be. Hard work also teaches lessons of perseverance, thoroughness, and many other character qualities which are important to cultivate.

A ministry mindset is also something I'm gaining from farm life. When you start farming, you aren't just growing vegetables; you are also growing customers, who soon become your friends. And this is something my parents have instilled in us; we are here not just to provide local, fresh produce, but to provide a different way of life, a new perspective, and we pray, a seed sown for Christ. To be a blessing has been the theme of their lives, and it is transferring to my own.

But, I think the biggest thing that farm life has taught me is trust in God. Numerous times I have wakened in the night, to the thud of hail on our roof. I get out of bed, and join my parents on our knees, pouring out our hearts to God, and pleading for his protection. When your livelihood is dependent upon something that can be wiped out in one hailstorm, there is nothing else you can do. Many times God has extended his hand of mercy, whether it was hail or frost, and miraculously protected our crops. These experiences strengthen your faith tremendously. And if God does not choose to answer our prayers for whatever reason, as we have also experienced, it teaches you not to question why, but to trust. These lessons transfer over to other situations in life, and have proved invaluable to me.

There are some hardships to farming, but many of these can be looked at as blessings as well. And for me, any hard things are outweighed with the many blessings. Finances have been quite tight through the years, and we had one particular winter that we call our "long winter." We ate mostly tomato soup and pop-corn. But we children didn't think it was too bad, because we all love tomato soup and popcorn! So it wasn't nearly as hard for us as it probably was for our parents.

Another thing that has been a little hard for me over the years, is that we haven't had the freedom to travel as much as we may have liked. Whether it's the fact that there are crops to be tended, or the pocket book is tight, the farm does tie you down. So we may not have been able to take exotic vacations, but my parents have tried to substitute that with more family time—which isn't so bad.

When you think of the typical family farm, there is often a sad trend; the children leave as soon as possible and want nothing to do with that way of life. I think one of the big reasons is because they have another life, a life outside of the farm circle, one of school and friends, and the farm only "hinders" that other life. For us this has not been a problem. The farm is our life! It's the place we spend the majority of our time, and the place we love to be! But this love for the farm is a product of my parents' choice to make the farm our sphere of influence. This is very important.

For me, growing up on the farm has been a rewarding experi-ence. I have always valued it, and appreciated the sacrifice my parents have made to make it a reality. I have enjoyed learning about the gardening process, but it was never a real passion of mine. I couldn't envision ever wanting to do it as a life work. That is until recently. The apprenticeship program has had a big part in this. I can say now, I have a real passion for gardening. It is something I love! And as this love has been planted in my heart, along with it has come a burden to see other young people with this same passion and vision for sustainable agriculture.

Not only is it an amazing character building experience, but a huge witnessing and ministry opportunity. We, as Adventists, have dropped the plow, and it's time to pick it up again.

In closing I wanted to share a poem by George Henderson from his book entitled *The Farming Ladder* that expresses his love for their farm in a neat way. It says,

> *Oh, little valley, all our own,*
> *Here is the place where beauty dwells,*
> *And all the joys this world has shown,*
> *Your gift of quietness excels,*
> *Nor would I change your streams and trees—*
> *For jewels of the Seven Seas.*

And truly, I wouldn't trade the experience of growing up on a farm, for *all* the jewels of the seven seas.

* * * * * * * * * *

Kirsten is now grown, and married to a wonderful young man. Nick Knecht came to us as an apprentice, fell in love with farm life, and then with the farmer's daughter. Their farm wedding was an amazing testimony to the blessings of the agrarian life. They see themselves continuing to live a life of agriculture on some level, and currently are still involved with the marketing at Bountiful Blessings Farm as well as doing some flower farming. They have built an adorable Tiny House that is currently parked in a quiet corner of the farm, but can travel with them wherever God leads. You can read their story at www.nickandkirsten.us.

Meeting his mentor

John has always considered Eliot Coleman to be his farming mentor. Eliot's work for small farms and winter production was unrivaled when we began farming. When Kirsten was fifteen, we heard that Eliot was coming to our area to speak, but it was on the Sabbath, the day God asks us to lay all our business cares aside. John was very disappointed to miss out on this opportunity to meet Eliot, but wasn't willing to compromise his convictions. So, Kirsten got it in her mind to write Eliot, explaining that our family had a small farm in Middle Tennessee where her father had followed many of his ideas. Since we were Sabbath keepers, and would not be attending the Saturday conference, she wondered if there was any time on another day that her dad could meet him. This hand-written letter was soon answered with an e-mail saying he would love to meet John for breakfast on Sunday morning, and he hoped Kirsten would join them. It gave Kirsten great joy to present this gift to her father! John and Kirsten took Edwin with them, and they had a wonderful breakfast "date"—talking about what they all love—farming. Eliot invited them to come and see his farm. This was very generous, but seemed quite impossible at that point. There was no money in the budget for a trip to Maine.

The following summer, we had a week-long seminar on the farm. At the end, one of the participants handed John a check, saying it was to be used for him, Jonathan, Edwin, and Paul to make a trip to visit Eliot's farm. These generous friends felt it would be very beneficial to our own production to see his farm in action—which in turn would bless others. At first Kirsten was a bit disappointed that it had been earmarked. Jonathan was not as interested in farming as she was. In fact, that summer he had opened Mighty Power Small Engine Repair. Why had they designated it as a father/son trip? Recognizing there must be a reason, we all came to peace about it, trusting that our friend's generosity had been led of God in every detail.

Plans were laid, and in the fall of 2009 the men flew up to spend a couple of days with the Coleman's. It was on this trip that Eliot challenged Jonathan with the idea of a mechanized baby greens harvester. Eliot is always thinking of new tools that can make small farming more efficient and profitable, but he's too busy farming to actually make them. Instead, he shares the ideas with others. He gave Jonathan a scrap of paper with a pencil drawing and Jonathan went home with the proverbial wheels spinning. Could this be why Jonathan was on the trip?

Within the first year Jonathan had a crude prototype, but at some point we realized he really needed the help of an engineer to take it from there to production. John and I had no more than expressed our need to make it a matter of prayer when God answered. "Before they call, I will answer; and while they are yet speaking, I will hear" (Isaiah 65:24). The very next day we had a longtime acquaintance at our farm. She and a couple friends came out to see the farm and share a meal. Just as they were leaving the thought hit me that her husband was a semi-retired engineer who loves gardening. I mentioned that Jonathan had some tool ideas and wondered if her husband would be willing to look at them and give him some ideas. Thus began a cooperative adventure that was more than we could have asked or hoped for.

That retired gentleman took a real interest in Jonathan and his project! They worked hand in hand for the next couple of years. In March of 2012, John and Jonathan returned to Eliot's farm to demonstrate the greens harvester. It was thrilling for them to see Eliot's excitement. The tool manager from Johnny's Selected Seeds was also visibly impressed as they tried out the harvester. That fall, Jonathan signed an exclusive contract with Johnny's to sell his "Quick Cut Greens Harvester." Who could have orchestrated such a plan? God alone! It gives us great joy to know that God is using Jonathan's talents to promote the healthy farming lifestyle and make small farms more profitable all over the world. You can see what is currently happening with his business at www.farmersfriendllc.com

More about family

All of our children have benefited from farm life. Their days were not controlled by school, sports, parties, or friends. They are not lacking in friends, but most of their socializing was centered in the family and on the farm. The farm was their life. Work was the norm. Play was earned. We praise God they have embraced the good in this sterner-than-normal life and recognize the value in it.

Joshua is following in John's footsteps. He loves the farm life and especially the care of animals. When his hens see him coming, they get all excited and flock around him like he's their hero. Of course, it helps that he has a bag of feed slung over his shoulder! For now he sees the life he's grown up with as just where God wants him. He is daily learning from the wisdom of his father, taking more leadership on the farm, and branching out into some personal farming endeavors.

It was the summer after John quit teaching (1997) that Zachariah was born in Oregon. It took years of God's guiding in Zack's life to bring him into our family. He was seven years old when we first met, and it was love at first sight. His inquisitive blue eyes were full of wonder. Just before his thirteenth birthday we learned that Zack was going to need a new home. God made it crystal clear to John that we should invite Zack to join our family. The rest of us agreed wholeheartedly. What a wonderful reminder that we too can (and need to) be adopted into the family of God! The Lord knew we needed Zack and he needed us. We praise God for bringing him into our family!

The farm has been exactly what Zack needed. Maybe it's just what all boys need! He has had many opportunities to learn the practical skills of life. He, like Jonathan, seems to be drawn to the mechanical side of things. Vehicle maintenance, equipment upkeep, small engine work; all these things interest Zack. His skills are growing. We know that God has a perfect plan for his life. In God's time He will reveal just what that plan is. Until then, he is learning to do whatever his hand finds to do with all his might.

Caleb is our fifth lover of the outdoors! He's also our wood worker—spending any spare minutes he can find in his shop. On the wall hangs a picture of his mentor, who worked in a little shop in the village of Nazareth. It's an amazing thing to see the way God gives children different talents and interests. As parents, it's ours to cultivate those talents, and encourage them to use and develop all of their abilities. This makes them more useful wherever God calls them.

From a young age we have encouraged our boys to be entrepreneurial so that they can be business owners and not just employees. Ideally these businesses are home-based. They have all had side-businesses that they managed alongside the family farm. It is our belief that real men are needed to lead out in their families. That takes much time; time for working together, doing hard things together, using common sense together, tackling the "impossible" together. Then, when the work is done, there's the reward of jumping in the pond, playing tag, or chasing a Frisbee. In a world of fractured and splintered families we have chosen the "old path where is the good way" (Jeremiah 6:16). We are confident that, just as God has led John and me, He will lead our children as they start their own families.

One more providence of God

After thirteen long and hard years of farming, the Lord laid on our hearts the need to have a Sabbatical—a time of sustained rest, reflection, and family. By then the farm was a very busy place with a constant flow of visitors. In many ways this was a great blessing—there was no need to go away from the farm to socialize. But we were tired and felt the need to rest. This simply wouldn't happen at home.

We rested in the fact that God was guiding us to take this time away. Through His word, and impressions on our hearts, we were confident of His leading. Now we watched for those providences that would open the doors and make the sabbatical a reality. We did not have much in the way of savings to rely on, but God doesn't need our savings to accomplish His will.

We pursued several possibilities where we could "house sit," but none of those opened up. One day the thought came to me that we should consider going back to Honduras. I was excited about this idea and so were the children, but for some reason John didn't see it as a viable possibility. After thinking and praying about it some more, I asked John if I could at least contact the missionaries there and see if there was even a possibility for us to take our Sabbatical at the mission. With John's permission, I made the contact. The response quickly came, and it was more than we could have hoped for. They would love to have us come! They even talked to the young woman who had been our translator. She was recently married, and her husband owned a small home on the outskirts of the village. The house was sitting empty and they offered it to us *rent free!* We all felt confident that this was the open door we were looking for. The finances fell into place, tickets were purchased, and plans were laid.

On October 16, 2011 we boarded the plane and our Sabbatical began. For the next three months we lived a quiet, simple village life. Very little Internet, no cell phones, almost no company; the language barrier added to the quietness. Each of us washed our own clothes by hand, wrung them out, and hung them on the line. The boys worked on school. In the afternoon it was not uncommon to see our family walking up the mountain to have some fun at the waterfall. The mission had a nice garden, and we enjoyed working in it. We rode the bus to town once a week to send and receive emails and shop in the open air market. The peaceful and uncomplicated life was exactly what we needed.

The local church took up a very significant part of our time there. Every Wednesday evening we strolled down the dirt road to attend prayer meeting. Every Sabbath morning we again walked to church, and then walked back home for lunch. Sabbath afternoons were spent in outreach to the community, ending up back at the church for vespers. We started a little choir with the youth and endeavored to teach them to read music, and sing in parts. Although our Spanish skills were very limited, we loved to join them in the singing. They loved to hear our family sing together, and said they could understand our Spanish pronunciation! Since the family structure is very weak in that country, just seeing a family together made an impact everywhere we went.

God appoints periods of rest, but He does not appoint total inactivity. He impressed both John and me with projects. This book was my project. Writing doesn't really seem like a Sabbatical project to me, but I knew God was calling me to testify of His faithfulness, so I was willing. My request was that my family would not "feel" me being absent and absorbed in writing. Family was the priority. If I was to write, it had to happen around the family. God was faithful. Since I was going to bed early, He woke me up early so I could spend time in His word, and then get a couple of hours of writing done before breakfast. God always has a plan!

God appointed that time of rest for us. We knew it would probably never happen again as a complete family. It truly was a precious time to refocus, rejuvenate, and recommit. We experienced revitalization, recreation, and restoration. We returned to the farm toward the end of January, ready to put our hands firmly back on the plow.

Our hope

Although our story is full of mistakes and often shows our lack of faith; although we grew weary and at times failed the Lord, He was faithful. We have proved Him, and we know that He *is* faithful to give us strength to follow any calling He places on our life. It is our hope that by sharing our experiences you will be encouraged to follow God's leading more faithfully in your own life. Wherever He leads you, whatever trials and challenges you encounter, know that He is doing a refining work that has eternal value.

LOOKING BACK

"What would you do differently if you were starting over again?" This is a question we hear on a fairly regular basis, and it is difficult to answer. The Lord used our particular set of circumstances to mold us and teach us just what we needed to learn. We do not claim to have learned His lessons perfectly, but they were tailored perfectly to our needs. In that case, how could we wish for anything different? I'm sure there are certain decisions we would change; specific actions we would love to re-do, but we are content to believe that God used *all* of those things for our good.

We are slow learners though! With all the information available today, there is no reason that someone should have to struggle through ten or more years of trials in order to "succeed" at market gardening. Then again, what is success? Were the early years a failure? I don't think so. My idea of success is laying up treasure in Heaven (Matthew 6:20). Success is finally hearing Jesus say, "Well done thou good and faithful servant . . . enter thou into the joy of thy lord" (Matthew 25:21). Anything less would be failure.

POINTING OTHERS FORWARD

Another question we hear frequently is, "What advice would you give to someone who is just starting out in farming?"

Again, that's hard to answer. How could we wish for anyone to miss out on the sweet fellowship we had with Christ through suffering? We look back on the hard years with a certain fondness; they drew us closer to the Lord and to each other! Would we want anything less for others? But how can we recommend something so difficult and uncertain? Do you see the dilemma?

The bottom line is that God wants to teach all of us total trust in Him. Farming is a very good "teacher," but there are others.

For those who think they would like to farm for a living, I would say:

1. Make sure it is a calling from the Lord and not something based on idealism or emotions. When the hard times come—and they will come, the knowledge of God's calling will carry you through.

2. Learn all you can from others through books, videos, farm tours, apprenticeships, etc. It's a lot easier than learning

from your own mistakes! There are many resources available now to shorten the learning curve.

3. Good books are available on the business of market gardening. These should be studied carefully; God expects us to use our heads. But our testimony is that we do best and find more joy when we focus on service and not on making money.

4. Fasten your seatbelt because you are in for an amazing ride! Just make sure God is in the driver's seat and you are keeping your hands off the wheel.

Our vision and dream

No, we don't think that everyone should follow in our footsteps, quit their jobs, and start farming for a living; that was God's plan for *our* family. But, it *was* God's original plan for man to live and work in a garden, and we do believe it provides the ideal environment to raise a family. Gardening should be a part of everyone's life, even if God has given you different talents and a different calling. Our dream is to see parents stop chasing after what the world calls success, make family a priority, cut back on work (away from home), step out in faith, secure a piece of land, grow at least some of their own food, provide meaningful labor for their children, work alongside them, teach them about real life, live simply, and learn to walk with God!

Pam's personal paraphrase of Hebrews 11

By faith John and Pam Dysinger left the "security" of payroll,
knowing God had called them to something better.

By faith they were patient in trial,
believing that God was preparing their family for Heaven.

By faith they sold their home in this world,
knowing that Jesus was building them a Heavenly home.

By faith John plowed the fields,
believing that God would bless his toil.

By faith they looked to the Heavenly bank account,
knowing God would supply their need.

By faith they saw the crowns of life placed on their children's heads,
believing God would give true success to their efforts.

By faith they looked at their debt,
knowing God would lift it.

By faith they set their eyes on God's reality,
believing He could change theirs.

By faith their hands are on the plow,
until God asks them to lay it down.

(Excerpt from November 2007)

How does God want **you** to fit into the faith chapter?

We invite you to view the complete
selection of titles we publish at:

www.TEACHServices.com

scan with your mobile
device to go directly
to our website

Please write or email us your praises, reactions, or
thoughts about this or any other book we publish at:

TEACH Services, Inc.

P U B L I S H I N G

www.TEACHServices.com • (800) 367-1844

Info@TEACHServices.com

TEACH Services, Inc., titles may be purchased in bulk for
educational, business, fund-raising, or sales promotional use.
For information, please e-mail:

BulkSales@TEACHServices.com

Finally if you are interested in seeing
your own book in print, please contact us at

publishing@TEACHServices.com

We would be happy to review your manuscript for free.

CPSIA information can be obtained
at www.ICGtesting.com
Printed in the USA
LVHW03s1330130718
583454LV00006B/84/P